What Senses Fail To Fathom... The Eucharist

SECOND PRINTING

Monsignor Frank Chiodo

What Senses Fail To Fathom... The Eucharist

Monsignor Frank Chiodo

Copyright © 2005
All rights reserved.

PUBLISHED BY:
BRENTWOOD CHRISTIAN PRESS
4000 BEALLWOOD AVENUE
COLUMBUS, GEORGIA 31904

INTRODUCTION

The Holy Eucharist is the crowning jewel of the seven sacraments. Although underestimated by many, the Eucharist has played a most critical role in the lives of true Christians since its institution by Christ, reaping results for the individual recipient in proportion to his or her faith. What we see with our eyes, what we taste, is only a sacramental entryway to wonders beyond the imagination. The lives of the saints throughout the ages give vivid testimony to the power of Christ's presence in the Blessed Sacrament, the Eucharist. At this juncture in world history, a world hungering for peace, serenity and solace will find a yet largely untapped power source in the Eucharist. The Eucharist is perhaps the most underused power source available to mankind.

Enclosed within the covers of this book are words which are designed to open up before us the wonders of a deeper faith, a more lively hope and a more profound charity enkindled by the flames of Divine Love present in the Blessed Sacrament. Our beloved departed Pope John Paul has invited all of us to come to a deeper appreciation of the Eucharist during this special year of the Holy Eucharist 2005.

The book is divided into three sections, corresponding to three themes which describe the Eucharist: The Eucharist as Sacrifice, The Eucharist as Presence and The Eucharist as Communion. The meditations under each heading are meant to elucidate for the reader the meaning and import of the various themes. Let the words and thoughts of this book admit you to a realm where you come to "grasp, through faith, what senses fail to fathom."(Words taken from St. Thomas Aquinas' hymn "Tantum Ergo Sacramentum.")

O SACRAMENT MOST HOLY, O SACRAMENT DIVINE, ALL PRAISE AND ALL THANKSGIVING BE EVERY MOMENT THINE. AMEN.

Dedicated to those faithful priests, who, through their example of love for and devotion to the Most Holy Eucharist and the Sacred Liturgy, have inspired me by inflaming my heart with a love for His Divine Presence.

The Reverend Monsignor Peter N. Schmitz, r.i.p. Pastor

The Reverend Benedict J. Kenkel, Pastor

The Reverend P. Basil Rechenburg, OSB, mentor and spiritual director

The Reverend Monsignor Frank E. Chiodo

TABLE OF CONTENTS

INTRODUCTION 3

Section One: The Eucharist as Sacrifice

CHAPTER 1
    WHAT AN AWESOME THING
    IS OUR FAITH! 10
CHAPTER 2
    TRUE HUMILITY 15
CHAPTER 3
    AN INSIDE JOB 17
CHAPTER 4
    A SPECIAL VISITOR 21
CHAPTER 5
    JESUS PERFORMED HIS
    FIRST PUBLIC MIRACLE 25
CHAPTER 6
    KNOW WHOSE SIDE YOU ARE ON 28
CHAPTER 7
    WE SACRIFICE WHEN WE LOVE 31
CHAPTER 9
    GOD SO LOVED THE WORLD 38
CHAPTER 10
    CHRISTIANITY IS A FAILURE! 40
CHAPTER 11
    BAKED BREAD 44
CHAPTER 12
    THE SIGNIFICANCE OF THE MASS 47
CHAPTER 13
    THE MASS IS A SACRIFICE 50
CHAPTER 14
    THE PERSON YOU ARE BECOMING 53

Section Two: The Eucharist as Presence

CHAPTER 15
    CHRIST IS PRESENT IN THE PRESENT 56
CHAPTER 16
    THE GREAT GIFT 60
CHAPTER 17
    THREE SYMBOLS – WHAT OUR
    CHRISTIAN LIFE IS ABOUT 64
CHAPTER 18
    A CATHOLIC MAN AND
    HIS MOSLEM FRIEND 68
CHAPTER 19
    JIM CASTLE AND MOTHER TERESA 71
CHAPTER 20
    IT'S ELEMENTARY 75
CHAPTER 21
    CHRIST'S KEYS TO REAL HAPPINESS 78
CHAPTER 22
    HELP AND HOPE 81
CHAPTER 23
    FAITH, LOVE AND PEACE 85
CHAPTER 24
    SO GREAT A SACRAMENT 88

Section Three: The Eucharist as Communion

CHAPTER 25
    THE MASS, WHAT'S HAPPENING? 92
CHAPTER 26
    DOOMSDAY CLOCK 95
CHAPTER 27
    MY HEART IS WITH YOURS 99
CHAPTER 28
    I STOOD WITH PETER 103

CHAPTER 29
>   REMEMBER THE ALAMO 107
CHAPTER 30
>   I HAVE A DREAM 111
CHAPTER 31
>   HOW FIREY IS YOUR FAITH? 114
CHAPTER 32
>   ONE OF ROME'S GREATEST WONDERS 117
CHAPTER 33
>   TURN DEFEAT INTO VICTORY 120
CHAPTER 34
>   KING OF HEARTS 123
CHAPTER 35
>   WHAT IS THE MASS? 127
CHAPTER 36
>   HUNGER PAINS 131
CHAPTER 37
>   WHO ARE YOU? 134
CHAPTER 38
>   WORRY 137
CONCLUSION
>   LITURGY OF THE WORD,
>   LITURGY OF THE EUCHARIST 140

Section One

The Eucharist As Sacrifice

The Eucharist as Sacrifice

CHAPTER 1

WHAT AN AWESOME THING IS OUR FAITH!

What an awesome thing is our faith! To realize what it is we really believe.

Take for example the Mass: Imagine Mary and St. John on Calvary that first fateful Good Friday 2000 years ago. If they closed their eyes as they stood at the cross of Christ and in their mind's eye saw all the Masses celebrated throughout history, what would be the difference between Calvary and the Mass? Imagine, if we close our eyes at every Mass, and, in our minds imagine Calvary and the crucifixion, what difference is there between the Mass and Calvary? None, no difference, the same essential sacrifice, Calvary and the Mass. The only difference is that the Mass is Calvary made present in an unbloody way.

The Mass, what an awesome mystery! Sometimes we get too close to the sacred and we become lukewarm and indifferent to the awesome majesty of it all.

I remember some years ago being in Jerusalem and standing on the site of Mt. Calvary and the crucifixion. On Calvary, next to the spot of Christ's crucifixion there is a silver image icon of Our Lady of Sorrows with the heart pierced with a silver dagger. I thought: A dagger pierces the heart of Mary by those who are indifferent and disrespectful towards her son's Eucharistic presence, whose hearts have hardened to its meaning. Stats: One third believe in the true presence. Behold the Lamb of God, words before Holy Communion - Do you believe?

A non Catholic once admitted to a priest, "I am not a Catholic, but if I believed what you Catholics say you believe about the Mass, I would crawl on my knees to be there every day.

At the Mass, as Christ's blood was poured out on Calvary, so His mercy, healing and love are poured out here and now.

I was reading the other day about a healing of a young 18 year old girl who had been a prostitute, a heroin addict and was going blind - She was hard and bitter. Some people convinced her to go with them to Mass. She didn't want to be in the church but she went. Suddenly, during the Mass, she began to cry. She hadn't cried since she was 13, and she couldn't stop. When she walked out the church door she said, "Oh God, I wish I could believe." At that moment she had her sight back, she was freed from the heroin as well and never had a moment of withdrawal. She said later, "I know what happened. At the moment Christ came, when the bread and wine changed into Jesus, I was changed." This is the power, the reality, the healing love that is offered to each one of us every time we come to Mass.

Everyone of us must ponder this question concerning the Eucharist - Either Jesus is present under the appearance of bread and wine or He is not. You can't have it both ways, and, if He truly is, then perhaps we should examine our understanding of how earth shattering and mind boggling that truth is.

Every day in the Mass, the Savior, Redeemer, Creator from whose fingertips tumbled planets, comes under the presence of bread and wine to nourish us, to heal us, to console, sustain and strengthen us...how awesome!

Have I become too close and comfortable with this truth that it has lost some of its power and impact? Then this is the time to open my eyes to the truth and its power to change my life. As the words of Jesus put it: Zeal for God's House consumes me ... yes, consumes me. This is my challenge and yours to be consumed with a burning love for Jesus, present in the Blessed Sacrament.

Just suppose that it was announced that Jesus would be at church next Sunday. The media frenzy would be incredible; crowds would clamor to see Him. You wouldn't be able to get in for the pushing and shoving to get close to Him. And yet, it is true, He is at every Mass and shall remain in the tabernacle, at adoration in the chapel to abide with you and never leave you, with his consoling Presence. What a time like this does for us is challenge our faith and to slow us down enough to see the relationship that faith has to love.

Sometimes we may wonder why we don't seem to take anything away with us after we celebrate Mass or receive communion or spend time in adoration of the Blessed Sacrament. The problem is our faith is too small and our love is too.

Someone once asked why he didn't receive many blessings from the Mass and someone answered, "Because your bucket is too small." We come to Mass carrying a bucket, like someone going to a well for water. We receive from the well only the measure of the size of the bucket. If you approach Mass or adoration with little faith and little love for Christ, you will only receive little. But if your love and faith in Jesus is great, you will take much home with you.

Sometimes we come and go from church unchanged and unmoved by the impact of His Divine Presence in the Eucharist. The problem is not with Him, it is with us and the small, shallowness of our faith and love. It is time to deepen our appreciation and love for the mystery of the Mass and the Blessed Sacrament through renewed love for Christ in the Blessed Sacrament. Either He is truly present in the Eucharist or He isn't. If He is, why is my love for Him as shallow and my faith as weak as it is?

Every parish has its story, its need for healing, its hope for a new beginning or a better future. Your parish can begin to experience a new vibrancy, a fresh outpouring of the Holy Spirit, (a dramatic healing where brokenness exists through a renewed devotion to the Blessed Sacrament.) As the young former prostitute was healed and began to see through the Eucharist, so your parish can be healed of its wound and begin to see a brighter future.

I encourage you to begin to gather the leadership of your parish and begin to plan, with your priests, for a formal program of

Eucharistic Adoration. Begin small, with a few hours each day or a few days a week. Provide time, with an unlocked church for people to come and to experience the powerful healing of the Blessed Sacrament. In the quiet, solemn stillness of the darkened church, God will speak to the heart and show you how to renew your parish and provide renewed strength and courage to your priests and a deeper faith to all of the members of your parish. I have seen the profound effects brought about by a Eucharistic Adoration program in a parish. Begin by planning for a renewed Eucharistic Life during this year Pope John Paul calls the Year of the Eucharist.

A man's daughter had asked the local pastor to come and pray with her sickly father. When the pastor arrived, he found the man lying in bed with his head propped up on two pillows and an empty chair beside his bed. The pastor assumed that the old fellow had been informed of his visit. "I guess you were expecting me," he said. "No, who are you?" the man said. "I'm the new associate at your local church," the pastor replied. "When I saw the empty chair I figured you knew I was going to show up." "Oh yeah ... the chair," said the bedridden man. "Would you mind closing the door?" Puzzled the pastor shut the door. "I've never told anyone this, not even my daughter," said the man. "But all of my life I have never known how to pray. At church I used to hear the pastor talk about prayer, but it always went right over my head. I abandoned any attempt at prayer." The old many continued, "Until one day, about four years ago, my best friend said to me, 'Joe, prayer is just a simple matter of having a conversation with Jesus."

Here's what I suggest. Sit down on a chair and place an empty chair in front of you and, in faith, see Jesus on the chair. It's not spooky because he promised, "I'll be with you always." Then just speak to him and listen in the same way you are doing with me right now. So I tried it and I've liked it so much that I do it a couple of hours every day. I'm careful though, if my daughter saw me talking to an empty chair, she would either have a nervous breakdown or send me off to the funny farm." The pastor was deeply moved by the story and encouraged the old guy to continue on the journey. Then he prayed with him and returned to the church. Two nights later the daughter called to tell the pastor that her daddy had died that afternoon. "Did he seem to die in peace?" he asked. "Yes, when I left the house around two o'clock, he called me over to his bedside, told me one of his corny jokes and then kissed me on the cheek. When I got back from the store an hour later, I found him dead. But there was something strange, in fact, beyond strange, kind of weird. Apparently, just before Daddy died, he leaned over and rested his head on a chair beside the bed."

When you look at the Eucharist, remember---there is much, much more than an empty chair there.

The Eucharist as Sacrifice

CHAPTER 2

TRUE HUMILITY

At the Last Supper, Christ wanted to show us to what great lengths he would go in order for us to understand and believe in Him. He washed the feet of His disciples. He stooped down and emptied Himself once again of His Divine prerogatives. No God stoops before His creatures, yet Christ wants us to understand that He loves us to the point of taking the position of a servant whose job is to bathe the feet of the guests. He even washes the feet of His traitor, Judas. That is how far God will go in order for us to believe in Him.

What does Christ have to do in order for us to believe? When we say: "Jesus Christ is Lord"– we mean among other things that Christ can cope with any situation. He can handle any crisis. Why? The reason is because He is present to us in the present. He is the ("Great I Am.") I am present with you – as the one who serves, who humbles Himself by washing the disciples' feet, who humbles Himself to come to us under the appearance of bread and wine. I am present with you in the Eucharist as your bread of life and your cup of salvation. What do I have to do in order for you to believe?

A Priests Prayer for Holy Thursday
Renewal of Priestly Commitment, Holy Thursday 1990

Come, O Holy Creator Spirit! Give us a firm grasp of the profound truth about Jesus Christ's priesthood. We adore and worship the one "who entered once and for all into the holy place with His own blood, thus securing us an eternal redemption."

Jesus – Incarnate God, God in the flesh, you loved your own in the world and you loved us to the end. The measure of your love is the gift of the Last Supper: The Eucharist and the priesthood. Gathered together around this gift through the liturgy of Holy Thursday, I renew before God's people and before you O God my priestly commitment. I pray: "Come O Holy Creator Spirit, come and renew within me the Divine energy of love which you gave me on the day of my ordination. Come O holy life-giver, give me new life – a more abundant priestly life – a life which is so energized with power from above that others may be transformed by your ministry through me. Come O holy life-giving Spirit – make me worthy – make me grateful, make me whole. Amen."

The Eucharist as Sacrifice

CHAPTER 3

AN INSIDE JOB

I read the other day about the way worms get into apples. Did you know that the worm does not burrow into the apple from the outside? According to those who study such things, the worm comes from the inside. An insect will lay an egg in an apple blossom, and later the egg will hatch. The worm will then begin to eat its way out of the apple. The thought occurred to me: "Evil is born in the heart of a man and woman and then, like the worm in the apple, makes its way out to cause its damage."

Lent is the time to get to the heart of the matter. To begin to understand that the Christian life is an inside job...Christ wants to work from our inside out- He wants to have our hearts. In the gospel story, Jesus is transfigured before His disciples. His face shone like the sun and His clothes became white as light. What Jesus was showing His three disciples was His inside – He was manifesting His Divinity- that He was truly God. And what Christ wants to do for us during Lent – is to get inside us – into our hearts, our souls and to make us completely His. My sisters and brothers, yes, Christianity is an inside job, and it is imperative that we acknowledge the fact that like the worm, that burrows its way out from the center of the apple, so there is evil which lurks in our hearts...and Lent is the time God has given us to have our insides changed...to have a spiritual heart transplant.

The year was 700 AD, the place Lanciano, Italy...a priest celebrates the Mass. This particular priest has had heart problems. Not physical heart problems, but spiritual ones. His faith in

Christ has been waning- the fire of faith has grown dim within. During the most sacred moment in the Mass, when the priest bends over the bread, this priest began to have doubts as to the true presence of Christ in the Eucharist. And when He once again uttered those anointed words of Jesus over the bread, something miraculous occurred. "This is my body" the priest pronounced...and suddenly the Eucharist Host began to bleed. The texture of the Host began to change - It began to turn into what looked like human flesh. The wine had turned into Blood. The priest's faith was restored that day. The miracle of Lanciano is still seen today – in the church there. In a golden urn are the remains of that Eucharistic host – turned to flesh and blood. In 1970, Italian medical doctors and scientists were invited by church authorities to examine the blood and the host. The results of the tests are stunning:

1. The flesh is real human flesh and the blood real human blood.
2. The flesh consists of a finely dissected tissue from the human heart.
3. In the blood was found proteins and minerals as in fresh shed human blood.
4. The flesh and blood have been in a natural state – for 1300 years. Normally blood loses its qualities quickly through decay.

The miracle of Lanciano has been accepted by the church as attesting to the true presence of Christ's Body and Blood under the appearance of Bread and Wine in Communion. Christ is in the Mass – and when He comes to you in Communion, know that He is giving you His heart – He is coming into your soul, so that He can change your heart – making it more like His own. He is changing you on the inside, and me too; and oh, how we need a change!

I was reading about 3000 high school juniors and seniors who were at the top of their class – when asked: 78% admitted cheating and 89% admitted cheating was common at their schools. One professor commented: "The numbers are disturbing, but even more alarming is the attitude." There's no remorse. For students, cheating is a way of life. Politically correct advocates tell us that truth really depends on your point of view. One person's truth is supposed to be just as good as another's. One thing we all need to restore to our lives is honesty and truth. Truth about ourselves – I am a sinner. A change of heart begins with me and you. We can't wait for Washington or the state house to begin to change – we need to change—by inviting God to come into our hearts today and to change us. Where there is dishonesty, may God make me honest. Where there is irresponsibility, may God make me responsible for doing what is right. May the only truth I stand for or live by be that saving truth of Jesus Christ, my savior and Lord present in the Holy Mass.

During the times of the knights of the roundtable, the candidate for knighthood would spend the entire evening praying in the church before partaking of the Blessed Sacrament. During the ceremony the next day, the knight would kneel before the king and place his folded hands between the two hands of the king…and would pledge his loyalty to the king with these words, with his hands in the hands of the king: "O King, I am your man." When we come to Mass, we should be saying and doing the same. We should be placing our lives in the hands of God and pledging our renewed loyalty to Jesus. We look into the eyes of Jesus at the Mass and we should say: "O King, I am yours. I am your man…I am your woman. May my heart belong to you forever. May your heart be forever mine."

This world of ours is in need of people whose hearts are one with Christ's. We can't wait for someone else to do it…we have to begin to take seriously our commitment to Christ, which comes from the heart. Our society is quickly losing its heart--its inner sense of good and evil--its basic instinct for what is just and right.

In 1996, Mohammad Jaberipour, 49, was working a route in south Philadelphia in a Mister Softee ice cream truck when a 16 year old tried to rob him. Jaberipour refused and the youth shot him. As the father of three lay dying, neighborhood teenagers laughed and mocked his agony in a rap song they composed on the spot: "They killed Mr. Softee." They sang…

"It wasn't human," another ice cream truck driver, a friend of the slain man who came on the scene shortly after the shooting, told the daily news: "People were laughing and asking me for ice cream. I was crying…they were acting as though a cat had died, not a human being." Now is the time to change our hearts and to begin to bring a new heart to the heartlessness of the age in which we live. Will you give Christ your heart today? Cry out "Jesus I am your man! Change my heart O Lord, Make it ever true. Change my heart O Lord, may I be like you."

The Eucharist as Sacrifice

CHAPTER 4

A SPECIAL VISITOR

Some years ago I received a very special visitor, his name was Fr. Lawrence Jenko. Most of us remember him as one of the Americans held hostage by the Moslem extremists in the early 80's in Lebanon. He was here visiting a priest friend who was living here at the time. He told many stories of his months in captivity. For much of that time the Muslims kept him locked up in a closet. He could barely see amid the darkness.

He told this story. Making a knotted string calendar, Fr. Jenko calculated the date of Easter and celebrated Eucharist in his closet. He said that he thought there was some poignancy in spending Holy Week as a hostage in chains. He said he retained a piece of the Eucharistic Christ, clinging to the Lord especially in moments of violence, sadness, boredom or fear.

One day he said he was holding Christ's body in a closed hand and one of the guards noticed and asked, "What do you have in your hand?" Opening his clenched fist, he showed him the small piece of Eucharistic bread and said, "This is Jesus." The guard stood in uncomprehending silence.

Sadly, it is often when we are deprived of something special, like the Eucharist, that we grow to appreciate its dynamic importance. How much do you understand and value the Eucharist.

As He sat at the table with His apostles on the First Holy Thursday so long ago, Jesus did something which continues to have it's impact to this very day ... He gave Himself to us. "This is my body given up for you," Jesus pronounced. And those words echo throughout the ages: Given up for YOU, given up for YOU, given up for YOU.

He gave up everything for us on the cross nearly 2000 years ago, but He continues to offer Himself to us every day in the Mass.

He saved us from hell on that First Good Friday and He wants to save us from hell now. Not only from eternal hell, but from the many other forms of hell humans occupy here on planet earth. Yes, hell. Some people are living in hell and can't or won't get out.

There are many in the world today who are creating a hell for themselves by enslaving themselves to meth, cocaine or to other drugs or drink, to sex, to possessions, and for them the words of Jesus especially apply - This is my Body, given up for you. Some others are held hostage in abusive relationships, violent, destructive and deadly. And to them Jesus speaks, "This is my Body, given up for you." Many suffer in various ways from the hell of loneliness, confusion, moral corruption, depression, sickness of all kinds. "This is my Body, given up for you," Jesus echoes.

To all of us and each of us, the Mass puts us in contact with the Savior, Jesus, who is made present to us under the simple appearances of bread and wine ... Why? So that He can save us from whatever hell we live in.

Fr. Jenko experienced first hand in the hell hole of a Lebanon prison, locked in a darkened closet, that Jesus is powerfully present in the Mass. Holding on to the little host after his Mass that Easter Sunday in Lebanon, he clung to the Lord, especially in moments of violence, sadness, boredom or fear. He knew it was Jesus alone who could save him and the Mass kept that truth firmly fixed in his heart. He understood Jesus' words, "This is my Body, given up for you."

As St. Paul puts it in I Corinthians 11: "For as often as you eat this bread and drink this cup, you proclaim the death of the Lord until He comes." It is through Christ's death that we are saved.

One author puts it this way: God not only became flesh for us years ago in a country far away, God also becomes food and drink for us now at this moment of the Eucharistic celebration, right where we are together around the table. God does not hold back, God gives all. The sacrifice on the cross and the sacrifice of the Mass are one sacrifice, one complete, Divine self-giving that reaches out to all humanity in time and space.

When Jesus hung upon the cross He cried out to his Heavenly Father, "Father, into your hands I commend my spirit." And when we raise the host, the Body of the Lord at the consecration, and the cup with His precious Blood, we should cry out with Him, "Father, into your hands I commend my spirit, into your hands I commend my body, into your hands I commend my mind."

Because Jesus gave Himself for us on the cross and because He continues to give Himself to us in the Mass in the Eucharist, so He offers us His strength, His power, His Divine energy, saving us from the hell of this world and the next. But we too must give ourselves to His Father, with Him, so that, with Jesus, we may be lifted up out of the darkness of our lives and set on a high place with Jesus, filled with a New Life and hope and peace.

At the next Holy Thursday service you attend, you will witness the re-enactment of the washing of the Apostles feet at the Last Supper by Jesus; understand what it means. It reminds us that Jesus lowered Himself to get on his knees before His own followers. But that was only a preliminary. During the Last Supper he lowered Himself in order to give Himself more completely to His followers under the appearance of bread and wine. All of this was a foreshadowing of His ultimate act of humility - His sacrifice on the cross.

At every Mass we renew within our own hearing the words of Jesus, "My Body is given up for you. My Blood is poured out for you."

Fr. Jenko showed the Eucharist to his Lebanese Muslim captor, and the guard stood in uncomprehending silence. When you see the host and chalice raised before your eyes, do you stare with uncomprehending silence, like the Muslim guard? Look with faith, with understanding, with profound gratitude for a God such as ours.

O Jesus we adore Thee who, in thy Love Divine, conceal Thy mighty godhead in forms of bread and wine. O Sacrament Most

Holy, O Sacrament Divine, all praise and all thanksgiving be every moment Thine.

Heavenly Father, you called your Divine Son to take up the cross and to offer Himself as a sacrifice for the salvation of the world. He was both Priest and Victim. And this call comes to every priest through the Sacrament of Holy Orders. On the First Holy Thursday you invited your Son's apostles to follow in Jesus' footsteps. And, to this very day, priests follow the same path as Jesus and His Apostles. Grant priests everywhere a fresh outpouring of the Holy Spirit, which renews and strengthens the grace of ordination. May the offering of our lives in the service of the church of Jesus rise like an acceptable sacrifice before you. With all the priests, who form a great army of witnesses to your love, I give you thanks and praise for this most precious gift - the priesthood of Our Lord and Savior, Jesus Christ, who lives forever and ever. Amen.

The Eucharist as Sacrifice

CHAPTER 5

JESUS PERFORMED HIS FIRST PUBLIC MIRACLE

In Canaan of Galilee, Jesus performed his first public miracle. Here Jesus changed simple water into a fine, fragrant wine. As you stand before the altar in the church built over the traditional site of this miracle there is a beautiful oil painting. Christ is pointing to the wine stewards, motioning for them to bring Him the water pots.

At the Last Supper, Jesus takes simple wine and changes it into His very Blood. Before the Last Supper meal, the gospel tells us, Jesus, God in the Flesh, changes his role and becomes a servant, washing the feet of his creatures. Changing things seems to be at the very core of the Mission of Jesus Christ. And Change is what God wants to do for us. But first we have to give ourselves to Him so that He can take us and change us.

Christ took water and changed it into wine. Christ took wine and changed it into blood. Christ took human flesh and became a servant, and Christ wants to take us and make us different ~ He wants to take us and make us one with Him.

In the church at Canaan, there is a small chapel a few steps below the main part of the church. There we found a large stone wine press. Here grapes were crushed in order to make fine wine. These wine presses were common in Israel at the time of Christ because people drank wine like we drink coffee or tea.

Change occurs in grapes when pressed and crushed - wine flows from crushed grapes. Change occurs in wheat when crushed - flour for bread is made; and change occurs in the Christian Life when we are crushed. Human life can be crushing pain, suffering, disappointment, loss, loneliness, fear - these are the grapes which can be the source of New Life. When we take our crushed and pain ridden lives to Christ.

If the stewards of Cana had not taken the water to Christ, there would not have been any wine. If the wine had not been made available for Christ at the Last Supper, there would have been no blood. If God had not become one of us, we would never be saved. And if we are not open enough to take ourselves and our bruised and disappointed and pain filled lives to Christ we will never be given new hope.

In Jerusalem, The Church of St. Peter in Gallicantu is built over the courtyard of the place where Christ was imprisoned the night before he died. Here, St. Peter sat in the courtyard and denied Christ three times. Peter denied his Master. And when Peter thought about it later he was crushed with guilt. I am a traitor, Peter thought. But when Christ rose from the dead, Peter repented and took his crushed self confidence to Christ and begged forgiveness and he was forgiven. Out of the crushed grapes of his guilt and sin, Peter was reborn, like a fine wine pressed from the wine press. New Hope was his.

But Judas, he betrayed Christ, handing Him over to the Jews to be killed. Later, he too was crushed with guilt. I am a traitor, Judas thought. But Judas failed to bring his crushed self confidence to Christ and he died, hanging himself from a tree in total despair. He doomed himself.

Who are you like? Are you bringing your fears, disappointments, pain, loss and sins to Christ so that he can give you new hope, or are you like Judas, keeping your crushed hopes to yourself?

This is the Mass. Coming to the altar to give yourself with your crushed hopes and dreams to Christ, so that He can change you and give you a new beginning - New Hope. "This is My Body," Christ says over the bread. And whispering he says, "This is My Blood," over the wine. And the bread and wine represents you. He takes you and blesses you and accepts your brokenness and your crushed dreams and changes you and makes you one with Him.

Christ lowered Himself to become man. He lowers Himself to wash the feet of His creatures and He lowers Himself again at every Mass when he reaches out to you and me. Pointing to our crushed hopes and dreams He says, "Come, I will change you like I changed water into wine. Come, let Me take you, as I took bread and wine, and make you one with Me, in my very Body and Blood." But, come you must, let Christ take you and, out of the crushed grapes of your life, let Him make a fine wine - a New Beginning.

The Eucharist as Sacrifice

CHAPTER 6

KNOW WHOSE SIDE YOU ARE ON

One of the most difficult things for us to do is to know whose side we are on and to act like it. A story is told of a man during the American Civil War. He couldn't decide which side he was on, so he wore a blue jacket and a pair of gray trousers. The problem was solved when the South shot him in the chest and the North shot him in the pants.

We have to take sides and stick to the right side. And, of course, the right side is always the side that God is on. We are all rebellious people to some extent or another. And, as rebels, we fluctuate between being on God's side and being on the wrong side, the side of wrongdoing and sin.

Holy Thursday is a day to recognize whose side we need to be on and to admit we haven't always sided with Jesus. Even the disciples on that first fateful Holy Thursday, when Jesus was agonizing in the garden, fell asleep, while one of them sold him for 30 pieces of silver.

My sisters and brothers, what the Lord wants from us is a resounding yes to Him. He never wants to hear a no from us. He wants us to say yes to everything that is His will. Yes to His way, yes to His Commandments, yes to His plan for our lives, yes to His plan for our families, our parish, our school and for the world. But we are all yes and no kinds of Christians and for this we grieve. In every one of us there lives a rebel. We want it both ways, you and I; to be with God and to be with the world - with sin, with wrongdoing and with pleasure seeking.

On that First Holy Thursday, after He had eaten the Last Supper, Jesus went to the Garden of Olives, and there he knelt in prayer. His Disciples slept, and He sweat beads of blood. There was a battle He was fighting, between the will of the Heavenly Father and the will of man. In the end Jesus cried out, "O Father, let this cup pass me by. But not as I will it, but as you will it." The will of God won the complete victory over the will of man, when Jesus suffered and died for us on the cross. And that victory is celebrated at every Mass.

When, at the Consecration of the Mass, the priest holds the delicate Host in his hands and speaks Jesus' words, "He broke bread," we are being reminded of how Jesus completely gave His human will to the Heavenly Father. What Jesus gave his disciples to eat that First Holy Thursday was the sign of Jesus' obedience and His Love for the Father in heaven. And when we are told to do this in memory of Jesus, we are being told to lay before God all hardness of heart, all rebellion towards Him or towards others and to say, "Yes," fully to all God asks of us.

When the Sacred Host is broken our wills must be broken and our hearts united with Jesus in one supreme, "Yes, yes, yes," to the will of God.

A Jesuit priest, Father Hunolt, tells a true story of two students who were talking about the hour of their death. They agreed that if God would allow it, he, who should die first, should appear to the other to tell him how he fared in the other world. Shortly afterwards, one of them died and appeared soon after his death to his fellow student, all shining with heavenly brightness and glory, and, in answer to his question, told him that, by the Mercy of God, he was saved and was in possession of the bliss of heaven. The other congratulated him on his joy and asked him how he merited such unspeakable glory and bliss. He said, "I am happy now because of the care with which I endeavored to receive Holy Communion with a broken heart." At these words the spirit disappeared, leaving his surviving friend feelings of great consolation.

The best way to merit the same joy that this blessed soul experienced in heaven is for us to understand what the Mass is all about. Standing on the side of Christ without reservation, breaking our rebellious spirits with the breaking of the Eucharistic Bread, crying out from our souls, with Jesus, as He did on the Mount of Olives, that first fateful Holy Thursday; "Father, your will, not mine be done." Amen. Whose side are you on?

A PRIEST'S PRAYER FOR HOLY THURSDAY

I have given you a model to follow, so that as I have done for you, you should also do."

Lord, you have given us a supreme challenge. You know how impossible it is for us to follow in your footsteps of kindness and compassion and service, but you do not order us without first offering us the power to fulfill your orders. Savior and Lord, on Holy Thursday, 2003, I surrender, into your hands, this parish. Take this parish with you to the cross, and there sacrifice it with you so that it can be reborn on Easter. I am its shepherd, and I pray you the grace to be a shepherd after your heart. Forgive me my imperfections and sins, my flaws and foibles, and grant an even greater outpouring of your mercy upon me and the flock you entrusted to my care. Break our hearts of all selfishness and sin, and open the floodgates of your merciful Love once again. May we all follow where you lead, do what you do and live in your life-giving Love forever. Amen.

The Eucharist as Sacrifice

CHAPTER 7

WE SACRIFICE WHEN WE LOVE

Isn't it amazing the lengths to which we will sacrifice when we love. Someone once said it well, "The greater the love, the greater the sacrifice."

I remember being in the Holy Land some years ago and visiting the two main bodies of water there, The Sea of Galilee and the Dead Sea. The Sea of Galilee is filled with sparkling water. Fish live in it, trees and bushes grow near it and people build homes near it. But, not far from the Sea of Galilee is the Dead Sea. Here, there are no fish, no green things, no children playing and no homes being built. Stale air hangs above the waters and neither man nor beast will drink of it.

There are two types of people in this world, the Sea of Galilee kind and the Dead Sea kind. The difference between the two seas is this: The Sea of Galilee receives water but does not keep it. For every drop that flows in, another flows out. The giving and receiving go on in equal measure. The Dead Sea hoards its income. Every drop it gets, it keeps. What kind of people are we? The Dead Sea kind, who take without giving back or the givers who remain fresh and vibrant by freely sharing of ourselves?

On Holy Thursday Christ gave Himself to his disciples in two ways that First Holy Thursday night. He gave Himself in humility in an act of Sacrificial Love when He bowed down and, like a slave, washed the feet of His followers. And then He gave Himself more perfectly under the appearances of Bread and Wine. And, in each instance Christ said, "Do what I have done."

How well are we doing? Am I a Sea of Galilee Christian or a Dead Sea Christian?

Bob Hope once said, "If you haven't got charity in your heart, you have the worst kind of heart trouble."

How's your heart? Like a river overflowing its banks, so the Heart of Christ overflows with love for us. At every Mass we join our hearts to Christ's so that, with the Bread and Wine, we might be changed into the very loving presence of Jesus in our world.

Mother Teresa of Calcutta puts it this way in describing the pathway Christ pointed out for us to travel: The fruit of silence is prayer. The fruit of prayer is faith. The fruit of faith is love. The fruit of love is service. The fruit of service is peace. If you want to truly know peace then walk this pathway. Spend time in silence and in prayer. You will grow in faith, and your faith will overflow into loving service of others, and then you will find peace.

Modern men and women seek peace in the heart, but they find none, because they look for it in all the wrong places. True peace is found in the sign of the cross. And, every time we make the sign of the cross, we are accepting the challenge of Christ, "Do This in remembrance of Me. Live the Mass by doing what I did, love others, give and you shall live in peace."

An old man collapsed on a Brooklyn street corner and was rushed to King's County Hospital. After some amateur detective work, a nurse located what seemed to be the man's son, who was a marine stationed in North Carolina. When the marine arrived, the nurse said to the old man, "Your son is here." The old man, now heavily sedated, reached out his hand feebly. The marine took it and held it tenderly for the next four hours. Occasionally, the nurse suggested the marine take a break, but he refused. About dawn, the old man died. After he passed away, the marine said to the nurse, "Who was that man?" "Wasn't he your father?" the nurse asked. "No," said the marine, "But I saw he was dying and needed a son badly, so I stayed."

I don't know if that marine was a Catholic or not, but I do know that, in the depths of his soul, he heard the cry of Christ made on that first Holy Thursday, "Do This in Remembrance of

Me. As I have done, so you must do." Do you hear the cry? What kind of Christian are you, a Dead Sea or a Sea of Galilee kind?

A PRIEST'S PRAYER FOR HOLY THURSDAY - 1988

Lord Jesus Christ, Bread of Eternal Life, Savior, source of strength, to you I offer praise and thanksgiving for the gift of priesthood. This gift, no one can deserve, I least of all. But you have called me to this ministry of Word and Sacrament. You have called me to speak your word, when convenient or inconvenient, whether the word will make me popular or unpopular. You have set me in the midst of this local church as its shepherd. I sometimes fail in this task. Human weakness and my own sinfulness cause me to fall short. I do not always live up to your expectations. Misunderstanding and hypocriticalness sometimes hem me in, but I must remain true to the duty you have entrusted me, come what may. Make me a shepherd after your own Heart, O Jesus. Give me a loving, understanding and compassionate heart.

Holy Thursday, some 2000 years ago, you gathered at a table with your twelve chosen ones. And there, you instituted the Sacrament of the Eucharist and called your apostles to pass on to posterity, this Memorial Sacrifice through the Sacrament of Holy Orders.

Eternal Father, this night once more I offer you the chalice of my soul, made holy by your anointing. Fill it with your strength, which made the apostles, martyrs and confessors. Make use of me in something good, noble and great for You, for your church and for the souls of many. I live only-- I wish to live only for this. Amen.

The Eucharist as Sacrifice

CHAPTER 8

WHEN WE DARE TO TRUST GOD

Several years ago Catherine Marshall wrote an article called, "When We Dare To Trust God." It told how she had been bedfast for six months with a serious lung infection. No amount of medicine or prayer helped. She was terribly depressed. One day someone gave her a pamphlet about a woman missionary who had contracted a strange disease. The missionary had been sick for eight years and could not understand why God let this tragedy happen to her. Daily she prayed for health to resume her missionary work, but her prayers went unanswered. One day, in desperation, she cried out to God, "All right, I give up. If you want me to be an invalid, that's your business." Within two weeks the missionary was fully recovered.

Catherine Marshall placed the pamphlet aside. She was puzzled by the strange story. It didn't make sense. "Yet," she said, "I would not forget the story." Then one morning Catherine cried out to God in words similar to those of the missionary, "God, I'm tired of asking you for health. You decide if you want me sick or healthy." At that moment, Catherine said later, her health began to return.

My sisters and brothers in Christ, there is a battle raging within each of us. It is the battle that has been fought from all time. Adam and Eve fought it and lost. Catherine Marshall fought it and won. It is the battle between my way and God's way...my way and God's will. Jesus Himself fought this battle.

On the First Holy Thursday, after He dined with His disciples, Jesus went to the garden and He wrestled with His will and the Heavenly Father's. There in the damp, clammy coolness of a spring evening, in the darkened shadows of the Garden of Olives, Jesus conquered His human self will. "Father, if this cup can pass me, let it pass, but let it be as you would have it, not as I."

Had the missionary not won the battle over her will, would she have been healed? Had Catherine Marshall not been victorious over her will, could she have been made whole? Had Jesus not cried out, "Father, not my will, but Your Will Be Done", would He ever have been saved?

After Jesus had washed the disciples' feet, He put his cloak back on and reclined at the table once more. He said to them, "Do you understand what I just did for you? If I washed your feet, I who am teacher and Lord, then you must wash each other's feet. As I have done, so you must do."

Jesus surrendered to the Heavenly Father's will and Catherine Marshall and the missionary did too. The roadway to this surrender to God is paved by many small acts of caring for others. Christ washed the feet of his disciples. This simple act paved the way to Calvary and His cross. When we put the needs and concerns of others before ours, we pave the way to our Calvary too. Our wills become obedient to God's will, our way becomes one with God's way.

And Jesus took bread and said, "This is My Body." He then took wine and said, "This is My Blood. Do this in remembrance of Me."

Bread and wine are two substances which tell us something about this surrender to God's will in our lives. No two substances in nature have to suffer more to become what they are than bread and wine. Wheat has to pass through the rigors of winter, be ground beneath the Calvary of a mill and then subjected to the purging fire before it can become bread. Grapes, in their turn, must be subjected to the Gethsemane of a wine press and have their life crushed from them to become wine. Bread and wine symbolize the passion and sufferings of Christ and the condition of salvation. For our Lord said, "Unless we die to ourselves, we cannot live in Him." Jesus took bread and wine and changed them into Himself.

We take what looks like bread and wine, but are really Christ, and we become Christ's Body and Blood. And then, we turn to the Heavenly Father and say with Jesus who is one with us, "Father, not my will, but yours be done." But, before we can come to receive the Body and Blood of Christ, we have to be willing to be changed. We have to identify with the bread and wine. Like the bread, we must pass through the fires of destroying our self-will, putting God's will first. Like the grapes, our will must be crushed and pressed into the fine wine of surrender to God.

This identification with the bread and wine can take shape in simple ways. Suppose your marriage is under pressure - communication is eroding, you need help, but are too proud to ask for it. The roadway to surrendering to God means asking for help.

Suppose close friends tell you that you are developing a drinking problem – you deny it, in spite of the evidence. The roadway to surrendering to God's will means seeking help from a doctor.

Suppose a friend or a family member has hurt us in some way and we are holding a grudge against him or her. The roadway to surrendering to God means forgiving that person from the heart and treating him or her with care once again. The roadway to surrendering to God is a difficult road. It is paved by acts of self-sacrifice, forgiveness and peace. It leads to Calvary and then the empty tomb – New Life.

When you take bread and wine, which is the Body and Blood of Christ, remember you are the bread too, ground in the mill of self-sacrifice. You are the wine too, crushed and pressed in acts of love and forgiveness. The roadway to surrendering to God is paved by acts of humility, care, and compassion.

When we think of Holy Thursday and the Last Supper, we must not only think of bread and wine, but also a pitcher of water and a basin for the washing of the feet. This pitcher and basin also challenge us to surrender ourselves to be compassionate, to understand that we are servants of God.

John Newton was a slave trader who, after the Civil War, was converted to Christ and then became a preacher. While on his deathbed, a young clergyman expressed deep regret at the prospect of losing such an eminent laborer for Christ. The converted slave trader said, "True, I am going on before you, but you will follow. When you arrive and you look for me, I can tell you where you can find me. I will be sitting at the feet of the thief whom Jesus saved in His dying moments on the cross." He classified himself among the chief sinners, those servants of Christ, who had surrendered themselves to Him, putting God's will before their own. How do you classify yourself?

A PRIESTS PRAYER FOR HOLY THURSDAY PRAYER – 1994

O Jesus, Divine Master, model of humility, and source of Love; priests participate in a special way in your shepherding role. And, with your grace, we struggle in our attempt to lead your flock along the pilgrim way of eternal life. Once again, on the feast of the institution of the awesome sacrament of the Eucharist, I pause to recommit myself to you and to your ministry.

May the priesthood, which is your gift, be the means by which many hearts are touched, many bodies and souls healed, many minds set free from bondage and sin. Refresh the oil of consecration, which sets me apart, and anoint me once again with the oil of gladness, of gospel power and of peace. Make me a priest after your heart. Amen.

The Eucharist as Sacrifice

CHAPTER 9

GOD SO LOVED THE WORLD

God so loved the world that He gave His only begotten Son, so that believing in Him we might not perish but have Eternal Life.

God gave His only Son. That word **GAVE** stands out as a bold proclamation of what God is all about. God gave His only begotten Son. God gave us His forgiveness. God gave up His only Son's life for us. God gave us His love from the cross and God keeps on giving, giving, and giving.

And on the First Holy Thursday Jesus reached down and took bread and a chalice of wine and he gave it to His disciples. "This is My Body. This is My Blood." It was His very self. He was giving His apostles. His apostles were being asked to see what He was doing on Thursday in light of what He would do on Friday. In other words, Jesus was connecting the Last Supper with the Cross.

The epic movie, "The Passion of The Christ", focused on the cross, but connected it to Holy Thursday, the Last Supper. In so doing, it underscored the integral relationship between the cross and the Mass. Remember the scene after the scourging, Mary and Mary Magdalene drying up spilt blood? Why? They did so because they recognized the Precious blood, which was being shed for the salvation of the world, foreshadowing the Precious Blood in Mass.

At every Mass we should envision two events, the Last Supper and the Crucifixion, because they are one and the same sacrifice. What is the difference if you close your eyes and see the Last Supper and the Mass? What is the difference if you close your eyes and see the Crucifixion? No difference. They are one and the same sacrifice--only now, made present mystically here and now in an unbloody way, so that we can be sharers in the power of the Last Supper and the Crucifixion of Jesus. Jesus gave Himself in the Body and Blood. Jesus gave Himself on the cross for the salvation of the world and Jesus keeps on giving, here and now, in the same way for you.

On Holy Thursday, we should be reflecting upon the cross and the great price He paid for us. When we come to Mass, the price tag is on display. The price tag for you and me...it is the Cross.

There is a story about how a young boy learned about the expense of Christ's cross from his father. His father, who was called Easy Eddy, had been the bookkeeper for the infamous Al Capone. One day, Easy Eddy reached a decision. He decided that giving his son a good name was far more important than all the big dollars Capone was paying him. Eddy was ready to go to the police to tell the truth about Al Capone. He would try to give his son some semblance of integrity. More than anything, he wanted to be an example of goodness to his son. He testified in court against Capone.

In a few months, Easy Eddy's life ended in a blaze of gunfire on a lonely Chicago street. Eddy knew that giving his son his good name was the greatest gift he could give his son, the only gift really worth offering to his son. And he purchased it at the greatest price he would ever pay for anything, his very life. And that is exactly what Jesus Christ did for you and me.

What is Holy Thursday all about? It is about a supper. A gift of bread and wine becoming Body and Blood; a cross; the shedding of blood and your purchase and mine at the price of Christ's very life. It's all about giving, giving, and giving. Christ never quits giving...that's what kind of God He is.

The Eucharist as Sacrifice

CHAPTER 10

CHRISTIANITY IS A FAILURE!

"Christianity is a failure!" The renowned English author G.K. Chesterton once made that remark. He explained what he meant in the following statement: "Christianity appears to have failed, but the real problem is that it has never been tried. The trouble with Christianity is not that it can't remake the world, but that it's difficult." In short, the problem with Christianity is the Christian. That is why Christianity seems to be a failure.

The Christian is the problem with Christianity! And the root of the problem is found in many Christians today. The cause of the apparent failure of Christianity is this: Lack of persistence, lack of stick-to-itiveness.

Ignace Jan Paderewski made the most revealing statement to a group of music lovers after one of his piano concerts, "If I would neglect to practice the piano one day, I would notice it. If I would fail to practice a week, the music critics would surely notice it. If I would fail to practice for a month, you, my public, would notice it."

The simple truth of that statement should pierce our hearts. When I, as a Christian, neglect one of those essential elements in the Christian life, like the plant without water, I begin to wither. If I would fail to catch hold of myself, I begin to go through the motions of living Christianity, but my heart isn't in it. Eventually, the Christian life becomes a mere memory.

In the Book of Exodus we may catch a glimpse of our own lives. Moses has led the Israelites from bondage in Egypt. He climbs Mount Sinai to receive the Ten Commandments, while the Israelites remain below. Soon, they turn from God and create a golden calf. The Lord says to Moses, "Go down at once to your people, who you brought out of the land of Egypt, for they have become depraved. They have soon turned aside from the way I pointed out to them, making for themselves a molten calf and worshipping it, sacrificing to it and crying out, 'This is your God, O Israel.'"

How quickly the Israelites forgot what the God of Israel had done for them! They were ready to turn to another god. They lacked persistence. How quickly we forget what the God of all has done for us! Do you lack persistence? I believe that the problem with many communities is that they often lack stick-to-itiveness. And one of the key elements to this stick-to-itiveness is stick-togetherness. Persistence and community is what we are talking about.

When I was at the Leon, Iowa parish, we celebrated the 125th anniversary of the parish. A parishioner made a painting of a large tree with roots sinking deep into the soil. On each branch of this tree were written the names of every family in the parish. What a lesson! Like a tree, our faith in Christ is rooted in His Lordship. Like a tree, our faith in Christ must grow and blossom. It must never be stagnant and lifeless. And, as this tree of living faith grows, its branches reach outward and more and more members are added. If any branch severs itself from the tree, it withers and dies.

If Christianity is failing, it is precisely because of the unwillingness of individual Christians to stick together, to be the living, vibrant faith community God wants us to be. The Vatican Council puts it this way: All children of the Church should remember that their exalted condition results not from their own merits, but from the Grace of Christ. If they fail to respond in thought, word and deed to that grade, not only shall they not be saved, but they shall be more severely judged.

The Grace of Christ is the grace of stick-to-itiveness and stick togetherness. How can we be saved if we refuse to respond to this grace? How can Christianity succeed if we refuse this grace? Christianity is a living, vibrant, alive reality. If it appears as anything else, the fault lies with us.

I saw a T.V. commercial on care of trees. It provided the five principles for the proper care of trees. The same principles can apply to us, for we as Christians are related to each other as branches of a tree. The five principles for the care of trees are: plan, plant, provide, protect and prune.

The five P's of proper tree care apply to us: 1. PLAN: God has a plan for us. He wants to see us as a strong united force in this community. In the gospel, Jesus refers to John the Baptist in these words, "He was the lamp, set aflame and burning bright. A lamp burns itself out, in giving light it consumes itself. The true witness for Christ burns himself out for God." Together, what a radiant blaze we can be. God has a plan for you. It includes the other branches of the tree. 2. PLANT: The seed of faith was planted at your baptism, but, it can remain a buried lifeless seed unless we rend and care for it. This is the message of the Life in the Spirit Seminars. 3. PROVIDE: Like any living organism, our faith must be provided for by our efforts to keep it healthy and alive and growing. We provide nourishment for our faith in community. It is in community that the Word of God is proclaimed and explained. It is in community that the Bread of Eternal Life is broken and shared. It is in community that we become the powerful force for the world's transformation. Cut off from the tree, we wither and die. Community is where our faith is provided for. 4. PROTECT: If we do not protect our faith from the dangerous influences of a godless society, it will wither and die. One of the ways to protect our faith is to practice it in community. This community, in a special way, provides us with the shield of righteousness to battle the principalities and the powers of darkness. Try to battle them alone and you will surely fall. 5. PRUNE: Every now and then a tree needs pruning of dead, lifeless branches. What in our life needs cutting out in order for you to grow stronger in your faith? What in your community needs cutting out in order to make it a stronger and more alive organism of faith?

The five P's are the tools given in order that our faith may be alive, radiant, powerful and influential in our world: plan, plant, provide, protect and prune. Stick-to-itiveness and stick-togetherness, persistence and community –these are two pairs of essential ingredients for an alive faith. How unworthy we are of this great trust!!

God has called us to be His church/His community, but so often we have sinned. We have failed to live up to the responsibility, trying to do it alone, only to find ourselves withering and waning in our faith. If Christianity is failing, I believe it is because of our failure, as Christians, to understand the importance of persistence and community. It is up to us if Christianity is to succeed.

There is a fable which can be a reminder to us: When Christ ascended into heaven, Gabriel met Him at the gates. Gabriel asked Jesus what recognition the world had given Him and His Divine Suffering. Christ replied that only a few in Palestine knew of it. "But Lord," Gabriel protested, "The whole world ought to know. What is your plan, Master, for telling the world of it?" Jesus said, "I have asked Peter, James, John, Andrew and a few others to make it the business of their lives to tell others and those others to tell others, until the last person in the farthest circle has heard the story and has felt the power of it." "But suppose they do not tell others, what then?" Gabriel asked. Jesus answered quietly, "Gabriel, I have not made any other plans, I am counting on them."

He is counting on YOU!! Persevere and stay close as a community of faith, stick to it and stick together. Christianity appears to have failed, but the real problem is that it has never been tried. The trouble with Christianity is not that it cannot remake the world but that it is difficult. The problem with Christianity is the Christian. REMEMBER: Plan, plant, provide, protect and prune. Christ is counting on YOU!!! Amen.

The Eucharist as Sacrifice

CHAPTER 11

BAKED BREAD

Not long ago, along the brick streets of the Southside of Des Moines, Iowa, what was once known as little Italy, you could find dozens of houses with large stone ovens in the backyards. They were used for making bread. There is such a rich symbolism in the making of bread. It is not difficult to understand why God chose to communicate Himself to us under the appearances of bread.

The symbol of bread and how it's made can teach us the deep meaning of the Holy Eucharist. To make bread, you first take sifted flour, millions of tiny fragments. As many grains of wheat go to make bread, so we are many different individuals.

But what happens to these individual grains of flour? Water is added. Now there is one large body of dough. Through the waters of baptism, God takes us as individuals and unites us, joins us with others and makes us one body, his family the Church.

Then what? A little yeast is added to the dough. It makes the bread rise. The Holy Spirit of God acts like yeast in us. It gives us the power to raise our minds and hearts above the ho-hum, dull, colorless life so many lead and puts us in touch with the real power, the power of God present in our lives.

After the yeast is added, the bread is kneaded, punched and pulled to work out the lumps and make it smooth. A healthy self-discipline is so much needed in our lives. We live in a pleasure-oriented, comfort seeking society. But to be a Christian means to work out the lumps of laziness in our Christian lives, to work daily at prayer, and to daily practice the presence of God.

God is not far from any of us if we only have the discipline to notice. The final step in preparing bread is to put the bread into the fire for baking.

In order for us to become finished products, we have to not only receive Christ into our lives, but also be willing to be received by Him. In the Eucharist I receive Christ, but Jesus also receives me and here I must answer these questions for myself. Can Christ receive me as I am? Accept me and affirm me as I am? The answer is in the gospel -- the crowd gathers to hear Jesus. As the hours tick by, the crowd is hungry. The disciples wish to send them away, but Jesus asks what food is at hand – five loaves and two fishes. He asks for it; the little they had, he multiplied it and he fed 5000 with the five loaves and two fishes.

The lesson is this: Jesus Christ wants to receive us in Holy Communion, each of us. It is not just our receiving Him, but he wants us to be willing to come JUST AS WE ARE with the little we have and be willing to give all of it to Him and He will surely give us more than we deserve in return.

Do you want to be a more loving, kind and caring person? Come with the little love you have and give it to Christ in communion today. Let him receive you and your little love. He will return it to you in abundance. Do you want to be a healthy and whole person? Come with your fragile health, your illness, your problems, your troubles, your temptations, your struggles and give it all to Him. Let Him receive you today and make you whole. Do you want peace of mind and heart? Give Him the little you have and let Him show you what He can give you in return. He cannot be outdone in generosity, as the gospel story shows. But giving Him ourselves with the little we have is the key.

On Corpus Christi Sunday, a very old tradition finds Catholics gathered together for a procession of the Blessed Sacrament through the streets of the city. The custom reminds us of the truth that Jesus is not up there in the clouds somewhere away from us inaccessible, but He is here among us, walking the streets of this city, inviting all to come and dine with Him, to come to know Him, to come and be changed by Him, and to come and be fired up with His love.

Christ cries out, "Come and receive me as your Savior and Lord, but come also just as you are with the little you have and be received by me." O Jesus, you make us one body, as there is but one bread. Your Holy Spirit gives us power to see you walk the roads of our lives. May we discipline ourselves to notice you for you are never far from any of us. Help to bring all that we have and give it to you today. We know you will give us 100 times as much in return, for you cannot be outdone in generosity. O Jesus most holy, O Jesus divine, all praise and all thanksgiving be every moment Thine.

The Eucharist as Sacrifice

CHAPTER 12

THE SIGNIFICANCE OF THE MASS

The three kings traveled from afar to come and adore the newborn King. Why? Because they had the faith to recognize the momentous, earth shattering, nature of Christ's birth. Upon entering the house, the three kings prostrated themselves and did Him homage. Then they opened their treasures and offered Him gifts of gold, frankincense and myrrh. And so today, why did you bother to come here? Perhaps not from afar, but you came. Why? Is the answer any less obvious?

Sometimes we need to remind ourselves of the simple yet profound meaning of what we do when we gather here. One of the saddest truths grabs every faithful church goer every year. At this time: Christmas Eve, Christmas Day, the church is full, more than normal. Then, a few precious days later, it is business as usual, back to normal. Where did all those folks go? I don't know, but I do know this – they cannot to any extent fathom, comprehend or appreciate what happens here or they would be sitting here every Sunday and Saturday, not warming their beds or eating or watching TV. I think we have become too sophisticated and too modern and technologized to appreciate the utter majesty of it all.

Not long ago, over 70 percent of our people attended weekly Mass. Now it is barely 42 percent. For the first time since Gallup has done their studies, Protestants have outshone us in weekly attendance. More Protestants attend church weekly than Catholics for the first time. What's wrong with our people anyway? I will tell you what's wrong. Many of our people don't know the weight of a Mass. Do you know the weight of a single Mass?

A true story can illustrate: A certain Father Stanislaus from Luxembourg, Germany recounts a true story. How one day in his hometown, a conversation took place between a butcher, a captain of the guards and an old woman. An old woman entered the butcher shop to beg for a morsel of meat. Disheveled and very poor, the woman was scoffed at by the butcher. "Please," she pleaded, "I will go to hear Holy Mass in exchange for the small piece of meat." A hush fell over the crowd in the butcher shop. The butcher peered over the counter. "You propose to hear a Mass for me? I'd rather hear the jingle of your coins." "But I haven't a cent," the widow whispered. "Then I haven't any meat for you," the butcher shot back. "But," said the captain, "she asked in the name of God." "Then let God provide her meat," the butcher barked.

The old woman turned to leave, but the butcher had not finished taunting her. "Let us see how much meat I would owe you," he said. He tore a tiny corner off his finest tissue paper and read aloud as he wrote two tiny words: One Mass. The butcher held up the tiny piece of paper and with glee he laid the wispy scrap of paper onto the resting tray of his brass scale. He then flicked a piece of old dried meat on the other tray of the scale. He blinked, confused. The meat side had not dropped to lift the lighter paper. "Impossible," the butcher exclaimed, placing a half chicken on the meat's side. Still, the tray holding the paper stayed down. The butcher piled layer upon layer; steaks, chops, loins, burgers onto the tray, but this did not tip the scale. He put his finest cut of meat, no difference. Brushing past the captain, he swept heavy ribs up and placed them on the scale. They didn't budge it. "The paper outweighs his goods," a man exclaimed. This scale was checked last week and it tested sound. Something is wrong here. The captain lifted the tiny scrap of paper off the scale and a gasp went up as the meat crashed down with a thud. What can this mean everyone wondered? People began running in from the streets to see what the hubbub was about. The butcher turned the scale around so that the trays were switched. No sooner did the tissue touch the shiny brass tray then it lifted the opposite one. "This cannot be," the butcher yelled, "the Mass intention weighs more than these."

The stunned butcher looked at the old woman. He made a gesture of putting everything at her disposal. "Come every day," he told her, "You will never go hungry again." The woman smiled and tucked only a thin piece of meat into her bag. "Why only a small piece of meat?" the butcher asked her. "I was ashamed to take more," the widow told him. "Ashamed?" "I was ashamed because even though I never had given up going to Mass, I asked you only for a small piece of meat in exchange for it. You see," said the old woman, "like you, I too do not know the weight of a Mass." Do you know the weight of a Mass? Spread the word.

The Eucharist as Sacrifice

CHAPTER 13

THE MASS IS A SACRIFICE

December 7, 1941 is a day that lives in infamy. The day the Japanese launched their surprise attach on Pearl Harbor. One of the most moving sites there is the memorial to the ship, Arizona. It was sunk during the surprise attack, when 1,177 young seamen went down to a watery grave. As you stand at this hallowed spot, the message coming from a loud speaker puts you in touch with the meaning of your visit there. "How shall we remember them," the announcer asks. The answer comes, "Mourn the dead, remember the battle, understand the tragedy, honor the memory."

The sacrifice those young sailors made on that early December morning in 1941 was the greatest that can be made. They gave their lives. The tragedy of their loss and their supreme sacrifice stirs our hearts and challenges us to come to a fuller appreciation of what the Mass is all about, because the Mass is a sacrifice.

As those young men died in the defense of freedom, so Jesus Christ the Savior of the world died for our freedom that we might be free from sin and live for Him. At the Mass we do what we were encouraged to do at Pearl Harbor, in the face of the sacrifice made there – Mourn the dead, remember the battle, understand the tragedy, honor the memory. This time, it is another battle we recall, the battle Christ fought was not at Pearl Harbor, but on Mount Calvary. Not in 1941 but 33 A.D.

We understand the tragedy, that an innocent One would die for us, the guilty, and we honor the memory. When we celebrate the Mass, we honor the memory of Christ's battle with Satan, sin and death, and the victory He won for each of us on that fateful first Good Friday, so long ago.

The Mass bridges the time gap and puts us in touch with Christ's sacrifice. It is as if the cross of Calvary is uprooted and planted squarely in our midst so that we may honor the memory of Christ's victory by drawing near unto it, allowing that Blood which was shed there to trickle down upon us and wash us clean from sin. This is the Mass, a sacrifice offered 2,000 years ago, but eternal, its effects enduring until the end of time. For every time the Mass is offered, the drama of Calvary is made present here and now. The Mass is a sacrifice because Calvary was a sacrifice.

The Crucified and Risen Savior is present here in a way that He is not present anywhere this side of heaven, A father gave a beautiful crucifix to his little daughter and said to her, "Now tell me, Helen, what is the difference between the figure of Jesus on the crucifix and the Host which the priest holds up at the consecration of the Mass?" The little girl did not hesitate a moment. "When I look at the figure on the cross," she said, "I see Jesus, and He is not there. When I look at the Host, I do not see Jesus, but He is there." My sisters and brothers, this is the meaning of the Mass.

On the hillside on the shore of Tiberius, Jesus fed the five thousand. Jesus took five barley loaves of bread and a couple of dried fish and fed the multitudes. At every Mass, the Lord feeds us with His own Body and Blood so that our hunger may be satisfied. Our hunger for inner peace, our hunger for freedom from sin, our hunger for a love which is heartfelt and everlasting. The Mass is a sacrifice because it represents the sacrifice of the cross. It makes it possible for us to do what the announcer on Pearl Harbor urged us to do: mourn the dead, remember the battle, understand the tragedy, honor the memory and one thing more, celebrate the victory. The victory Christ won for us, giving us eternal freedom.

Not long after the Civil War, a caretaker of a cemetery noticed a man praying at a certain grave each week. In the summer the man would place flowers there. The caretaker asked the man one day, "Who is buried in this grave that he should deserve so much of your devotion and love?" The man replied, "This is the grave of a very dear friend of mine. In the Civil War he volunteered to take my place that I might stay home with my wife and children. He was sent to fight and he was killed in his first battle. He was brought home and buried here." Then with tears in his eyes the man continued, "Do you blame me for being so grateful to one who died that I might live?"

My friends, this is the Mass. Christ's eternal sacrifice is made present here and now. Christ died for us so that we might live. Someone once wrote about the Mass and the cross: Over the prostrate world rises the cross of our Savior, the symbol and the instrument of our salvation. As He hangs upon it in eternal sacrifice, torrents of grace and truth and love stream down from His open heart upon sinful humanity. This divine offering is ceaselessly repeated in the holy sacrifice of the Mass; from the rising of each day's sun until the going down of the same, over all the continents, until the end of time.

This is the Mass. What a gift! What a privilege to be there!

The Eucharist as Sacrifice

CHAPTER 14

THE PERSON YOU ARE BECOMING

In the novel, "The Man Who Lost Himself", the hero trails a suspect to a Paris hotel. To learn the suspect's room number without arousing suspicion, the hero gives the clerk his own name and asks if a man by that name is registered. While the clerk checks the room list, the hero plans to watch for the suspect's number. To the hero's surprise, the clerk doesn't check the list. He simply says, "He's in Room 40. He's expecting you." The hero follows the bellhop to Room 40. When the door opens, he sees a man who is his double, except that he is heavier and older. It is the hero himself, 20 years in the future. The story is science fiction, but it contains an important truth; there is a person in everyone's future. It is the person we are becoming.

What kind of person am I becoming? The Mass is a celebration of the new and better person God is calling us to become. The Mass can be called the "Great Becoming" as God became man at the first Christmas. As Jesus became present to His disciples under the appearances of bread and wine at the Last Supper, so Christ becomes present to us at every Mass so that we may become holier people.

In the letter to the Romans, we read, "We have been called to belong to Jesus Christ, beloved of God and called to holiness." The celebration of the Mass itself is a reminder to us of what God wants us to become.

During the Eucharistic Prayer of the Mass, we are drawn into the mystery of Christ's cross and resurrection and if we are open to it, we begin to become intimately related to our God. It is as if through this great prayer and the raising of the chalice, the precious Blood of Jesus drips down onto our hearts, bodies and minds, to cleanse us and to write the name of Jesus in His own blood upon our hearts. What a great and awesome gift is revealed to us at this moment of the Mass! It would be a blessing to begin to recognize what is happening when the Host and Chalice are raised up—between Heaven and Earth—as the cross was raised on the first Good Friday. In the scriptures we are reminded: "When I am lifted up, I will draw all to myself." Yes, He is drawing us to Himself, as He is lifted up before us in this solemn moment of the Mass.

As we are drawn up into the divine embrace of the Godhead at the elevation of the Sacred Host and Sacred Chalice at Mass, we should recognize that Christ wants to mold us and transform us into His own divine image. There is an old saying: "Be patient with me, God's not finished with me yet." It usually takes a lot of time for us to be transformed into that divine image. The lives of the saints remind us of the long and arduous road to holiness that we must all choose to travel. Every Mass draws us closer and closer to the Savior, and gradually, but ever so certainly effects the transformation of grace that the Mass offers the world. The Sacrifice offered on Calvary two thousand years ago is made present on our altars at Mass, so that with Christ we might die to our "old self" and be reborn in Christ's spirit of holiness.

If you were to meet yourself walking out of Church the next time you go to Mass, and meet yourself 20 years from now, what kind of Christian would you see? What kind of person are you becoming?

Section Two

The Eucharist As Presence

The Eucharist as Presence

CHAPTER 15

CHRIST IS PRESENT IN THE PRESENT

"How lovely is your dwelling place O Lord God of hosts"...I learned early in my life, the truth of that statement. I was in the third grade during a typically frightening April storm in Iowa. Having left the school building during a tornado warning, I took shelter in the church until the school bus arrived. When I finally found my way back to the school, when the storm abated, I was confronted by a group of frantic religious sisters. "Where were you? We were looking all over for you." "I was in church," I muttered. Then one of the nuns made a statement, the import of which has been seared into the very fiber of my soul. She said "No better place could you be during a storm than with Jesus in the presence of the Blessed Sacrament." Those were truly anointed words; I have carried them in my heart from that day on.

This basic and fundamental truth is one of the crown jewels of all the truths of our faith: Jesus is truly present body, blood, soul and divinity in the Blessed Sacrament. This is the truth not always appreciated, too often forgotten, sometimes underestimated, occasionally doubted or denied.

About an hour train ride from Rome, there is an ancient mountain town called Orvieto. Inside the Renaissance Cathedral in a side chapel there is enthroned above the altar- - encased in a golden urn - -a simple white cloth about the size of a handkerchief. Upon close examination you will detect what appears to be stains of blood imprinted upon the white cloth, now yellow with age. The story behind this blood stained cloth is this: During the middle ages in the nearby town of Bolsano, a priest was struggling with his faith. He battled with the issue of Christ's presence in the Eucharist. He came to the point where he could not believe that Christ could be truly present under the appearance of the simple wafer of bread. One morning as the tonsured priest stood at the stone altar of the Bolsano church reciting the words of institution, something fantastic occurred. As the priest leaned over the species of bread and solemnly repeated the words of the Savior - - This is my body - -the host he casually held in his hands began to ooze what looked like human blood. Upon examining the white cloth which lay on the altar under the host, the investigation revealed that it was indeed human blood which stained this cloth. It is believed that Christ who is truly present in the Eucharist revealed the truth of His divine presence in the Eucharist. Now the cloth sits encased before the public eye as a testimony to the unbeliever and the doubtful; it is a silent yet eloquent way of asking a basic question of the onlooker - - how much does God have to do to make you believe??? Really, there is nothing God can do to force us into believing that He really present in the Eucharist; it is only by our free choice that we decide –yes, I believe.

There is an old saying: "For those who believe, no proof is necessary; for those who do not believe, no proof is enough." But God chooses the simplest things in order to communicate the most mysterious of truths.

At the Last Supper, Jesus gave Himself away –He hands Himself out as a little piece of bread so small and insignificant. He empties Himself of His Divinity ---by coming as simple bread—in order to fill us with His love. Do you believe? A Protestant couldn't believe in Christ's presence in the Eucharist. The Catholic answered him with a question, "Isn't your God big enough to come to you in the form of a small piece of bread?" How big is your God?

One of the most poignant points made in the teaching that Christ is present in the Eucharist is that He is present in the present. The present moment is the time when Christ can be encountered. Christ lowered Himself by becoming man. Christ lowers himself still as He comes to us once again under the appearance of simple bread and wine. He is not a God out there or up there, unreachable and remote. No, God's ways can boggle the mind. He spares no efforts in attempting to teach us of His presence.

In a survey recently conducted we find that only 30% of American Catholics hold to the authentic faith that Jesus is truly present Body, Blood, Soul and Divinity in the Eucharist. How sad it is! God grant that we might find ourselves always in the thirty percent of believers.

Remember the story of Moses when he approached the burning bush on Mt. Sinai: Moses asked God what His name was and God answered, "My name is I am." This title for God –the Great I am, reminds us of the truth that God is present to us in the present. When our sorrows overwhelm us, He says I am present. When troubles threaten your peace, He says I am present. When doubts plague you, He says I am present. When we feel very much misunderstood, alone or forgotten, Christ says I am present. Christ went to great lengths to be present to us in the present – he is present to us as a servant – he wants to be of service to us in our struggles, our trials, our temptations.

Dr. Leon Winters is a highly acclaimed Chicago surgeon. One night he was awakened at 1:00 a.m. with a start. The hospital called – a young boy had a terrible accident. He was a skilled specialist in an area that could help save the young boy. The quickest route was through a rough area of town – but the doctor decided it was worth the risk. He almost made it through the worst part of the neighborhood – when at a stop light, his car door was jerked open by a man in a grey hat and dirty flannel shirt. "I've got to have your car!" the man screamed, pulling the doctor from his seat. Winters tried explaining –but the man wouldn't listen. The doctor waited for over 45 minutes looking for a phone. When a taxi finally got him to the hospital, an hour had passed. The boy had died. The nurse explained, "The boy's dad got here just before he died. He is in the chapel. Go see him. He could not understand why you never came."

Without explaining, Dr. Winters hurried down to the chapel and at the front knelt the form of a weeping father in a grey hat and dirty flannel shirt. The doctor remembered: he was the man who ordered him out of the car – tragically the man had pushed from his life the only one who could save his son.

Often we push from our lives the only one who can save us – we try so desperately to be on the spot to solve our own problems when Christ wants to be the only savior of our lives.

St. John Vianney once said "If you only realized how much Jesus loves you in the Blessed Sacrament, you'd die of happiness." The protestant said: "If I believed what you Catholics claim to believe about the Blessed Sacrament, I'd crawl to receive Him"

What does Christ have to do in order for us to believe? When we say: "Jesus Christ is Lord" we mean among other things that Christ can cope with any situation. He can handle any crisis. Why? He can do all things through His marvelous presence in the Blessed Sacrament.

The Eucharist as Presence

CHAPTER 16

THE GREAT GIFT

It was July 19, 1989. United flight 232 from Denver to Chicago was in serious difficulty. An explosion had crippled all three hydraulic systems that operate the mobile tail and wing parts and steer the craft up, down and sideways. Passengers were told to expect an emergency landing. The pilot aimed for the Sioux City, Iowa airport and an unused runway. The 168 ton craft cart-wheeled and broke into fragments that spewed across the runway into a cornfield. Of the 296 passengers, 185 survived. One of the survivors, interviewed shortly after the crash, remarked: "I was doing a great deal of praying before we crashed, thinking of my family and friends. In the final minutes before the crash, I wrote a letter to my family. I wrote what a person thinks should be written if the end is near. I finished the letter, shoved it into my briefcase, took off my glasses, removed the pens from my shirt pocket and put those into my briefcase. I noticed the nun across from me had been praying on her rosary. I pulled out a cross I had in my pocket. I held it in my hand for the rest the ride." I chose to share this incident and commentary from the crash of flight 232 because it underscores one all important truth: Practices we should never take for granted are the treasures of our faith – they are gifts. The sister seated on flight 232 prayed her rosary – it was an anchor for her. The man commented that he carried a cross in his pocket – this gift of faith was a source of courage for him.

My sisters and brothers in Christ: we so take for granted the critically important expressions and treasures of our faith—these special gifts are what see us through many a trial and tribulation. The most precious of expressions of faith, treasure beyond all price, the source or summit of Christ's life is the Eucharist. Have we taken it for granted? I remember hearing about prisoners during World War II. Prisoners would deprive their bodies of needed sleep in order to get up before the rising bell for a secret Mass...offered in some dark corner of a prisoner of war bunker. If they were discovered saying Mass - - there were always informers - - they would be severely beaten, starved or otherwise brutalized.

The Mass was a source of strength and courage – an anchor amid the tidal waves of Nazi oppression. The words of Jesus whirled and swirled in the hearts of those poor prisoners of war: I myself am the living bread come down from heaven. If anyone eats this bread he shall live forever: the bread I shall give is my flesh for the life of the world.

What does the Mass and Holy Communion mean to us? Does it mean as much to us as those prisoners of war? Deprived of it, would it mean more?

It was the height of the Vietnam War when a young recruit by the name of Scott Bailey arrived at his post at a place referred to simply as bridge #29. Bailey's lifelong desire was to become Catholic, and after arriving at bridge #29, he sought out the Catholic chaplain and began instructions. He would be sent out regularly on mission, but when he returned he always looked for the Father and took his latest instruction class. Finally the day for his First Communion approached, and although it was raining fiercely, the chaplain offered Mass in the rain-soaked mud below the bombed out bridge # 29. He wanted to wait for drier weather to have Mass and give him communion, but Bailey insisted: " I want with all my heart to receive my Lord in Holy Communion. It has been my lifelong dream." During Mass when the time for Bailey to receive communion arrived, he did something the chaplain never has forgotten. As the priest held the host up before Scott Bailey's faith-filled eyes, Bailey suddenly plopped to the ground and there in the mud soaked earth, his legs nearly buried in the muck – Bailey tearfully received his Lord in First Holy

Communion. In humble adoration, kneeling before His Savior under the appearance of bread, Scott gave witness to his belief in the True Presence of Christ in the Blessed Sacrament.

The next morning, Bailey went on patrol. A few days later, when the chaplain made his rounds, he stopped in an area of the camp that no one wanted to visit – as the priest blessed the bodies of the slain young, his mind returned to the night when Bailey made his first Holy Communion. When you come to communion the next time, think this way: if this were my first Communion, my last and only Communion, how would I approach this great gift? That's the attitude of faith.

Ryan Hardaman, another passenger on flight 232 remarked shortly after the crash: "When we first hit, I thought, 'I'm going to die.' I had never thought about it before. The dead bodies didn't seem real. I am going to go to church. Every Sunday I'll be there." Do we need a tragedy to jar us back to the realization that the Mass, the Eucharist, is the very presence of Christ, under the appearance of bread. It is the same Christ who was born in Bethlehem, the same Christ who died on the cross, the same Christ who rose from the dead. How precious is that treasure to you?

St. Thomas More is one example of a man who died for the tradition – he knew what God expected of him. Chancellor of England at the time of Henry VIII, he loved the treasures of our Church, especially the Mass. One morning while the Chancellor was worshipping his Savior at Mass, a message came from the King. It was urgent he was told. It demanded immediate attention. To the messenger More gave this reply to the King: "Tell his majesty to have a little patience, as I am at this moment engaged with a King who is higher than he, for I am celebrating Mass. As soon as my audience with the King of Heaven is ended, I will at once obey the desire of my Earthly King." Faithful to the Catholic faith, he died for it--dying a martyr.

Scott Bailey's first Communion was his last. Discover the fire of faith which burned like a blast furnace in the heart of Scott Bailey. Faith – cultivate it, protect it, proclaim it. When your faith in the true presence of Christ in the Blessed Sacrament begins to wane, when your mind wanders at Mass, and indifference creeps in, when Holy Communion becomes routine, when you are tempted to doubt the importance of the Mass, when the fires of love for Jesus in the Blessed Sacrament start to die out, think of Scott Bailey at bridge #29.

Receive communion each time as if it were your first, last and only Communion. Let your faith in the Blessed Sacrament grow deeper. Here is the most precious of all earthly and heavenly treasures. St. John Vianney said: "If you only know how much God loves you in the Blessed Sacrament, you'd die of happiness." O SACRAMENT MOST HOLY, O SACRAMENT DIVINE, ALL PRAISE AND ALL THANKSGIVING, BE EVERY MOMENT THINE.

The Eucharist as Presence

CHAPTER 17

THREE SYMBOLS – WHAT OUR CHRISTIAN LIFE IS ABOUT

Three pairs of symbols drive home what Holy Thursday is about and what our Christian Life is about: bread and wine, water and basin, a priest and God's people.

Bread and wine: Jesus says, "This is My Body. This is My Blood. Do this in remembrance of Me." This Jesus, who, through His life, broke Himself in many acts of self-giving. Jesus, who allowed Himself to be broken on the cross, sits with the twelve and breaks bread. This bread, broken for you is My Body given for love of you. This wine, from crushed grapes, is My Blood shed for you.

At that first Mass, Jesus gives us a dramatic presentation of who He is. He is the Lord, who has given His all for us. He stood broken on the cross. He continues to give His all every time we gather for the Eucharist. When we eat this bread and drink this cup, we proclaim your death Lord Jesus, until you come in glory.

In the gospel story we have the second symbol – water and a basin. Jesus, Lord of the Universe, Creator of the stars and earth. Jesus, from whose fingertips tumbled the galaxies and planets, took water and a basin, girded Himself with a towel, and washed the feet of His followers. The creator humbles Himself before His creatures, and then He says, "What I did, so you are to do." This is said to us as well. Not just wash feet, but humble ourselves in service to others.

Christ is pointing out for us the reality of His Presence in matter, in bread and wine and in human beings. The one great thing that we need to learn is that Christ is found in and amid material things – spirit through matter, God in flesh, God in the Sacrament. We adore His presence under the appearance of bread and wine, but then we have to come out from before the tabernacle and walk with Christ, mystically present in us, out into the streets of our cities and find the same Jesus in the people of our neighborhoods – that's the harder part. We cannot claim to worship Jesus in the tabernacle if we do not pity Jesus in the slums. We must go out and look for Jesus in the ragged, in those who have lost hope, in those who are struggling to make good – look for Jesus. And, when you see Him in there…gird yourselves with towel and try to wash their feet by loving them as Christ does.

Christ is present at home, in the wife or husband who has a need to be cared for, who longs to be spoken with, not spoken at, who longs for the love that was once so real and now seems like a darkened shadow of what was. Christ is present in the children who long for direction and receive none. (In the neighbor or relative who, for fear of our being obligated, or being required to go out of our way for them, Christ is present.) Sometimes it is easier to recognize Him in the bread and wine than it is in other people, but with the same faith, we must open our eyes and see Him.

We remember Christ in two ways: in the Eucharist and in Service, two in one. On Holy Thursday, these two elements of Jesus' life and our lives are dramatically celebrated; washing of the feet (12 parishioners) and the Eucharist. Later, processions with the Blessed Sacrament around the church reminds us that Christ is not out there somewhere in the clouds, distant and inaccessible, but He is in our midst daily, calling us. Hear Him speak, "Do this in remembrance of Me. Break yourselves, serve others. Do this in remembrance of Me."

Do this in remembrance of Me. Pour out your concern for one another as I poured out my Blood for you. Do this in remembrance of Me. Find Me here--the God of the Universe, under the appearance of food, simple bread and wine. "Behold," Jesus says, "I am here, on the altar and next to you. Do you have the faith to find Me in both places?"

There is a third pair of symbols – a priest and his people. In fact, three priests and the people they serve. Holy Thursday is a commemoration of the institution of the sacrament of the priesthood. On that night, Christ called His twelve to not only lead the people in the Eucharistic sacrifice, but also to lead God's people in becoming the Eucharist to the world –signs of God's merciful love and compassion.

To me it is an awesome responsibility, but a wonderful privilege to be a parish priest. May God forgive me my blunders, mistakes in judgments, and errors; but may He raise me up, in spite of them, to be the kind of pastor He wills me to be. Pray for priests. Pray for us. What beautiful symbols spoken. Bread and wine, water and a basin, priests and people. Thank you Lord for making us your Eucharistic people. Amen.

A PRIEST'S PRAYER FOR HOLY THURSDAY PRAYER – 1982

O Savior of the world, this day, the Thursday that we call holy, is the priest's special day. On the First Holy Thursday, seated with your disciples, you offered yourself, Body, Blood, Soul, and Divinity to the Heavenly Father, in anticipation of the sacrifice, which you were to raise up to the Father on the next day, the First Good Friday.

You told your apostles, "Do this in remembrance of Me." In these words is contained the mystery of the priestly life. I, one of your priests, am commanded to celebrate the passion, death and resurrection at the altar; leading your holy people in this supreme act of thanksgiving and praise. How unworthy we are. How unworthy I am.

"Do this in remembrance of Me." Here you tell your priests also to give of themselves in remembrance of Him who gave all. In these words you tell us, your chosen priests, to give our lives – body and blood in service of your holy people. How often we have failed you. How often I have failed you. Keep your priests close to you. Forgive me my failings, my inconsistencies, my sins. O Savior, Jesus Christ, you tell me, "Do this in remembrance of Me." May my life be a sacrifice of praise to you, on behalf of your people. May I always be faithful. May the seeds you plant through my efforts, reap a harvest in abundance, in the lives of those I am unworthily called to serve. Thank you for your priesthood. Amen.

The Eucharist as Presence

CHAPTER 18

A CATHOLIC MAN AND HIS MOSLEM FRIEND

In an article by Peter Kreeft, he recounts the following conversation between a Catholic young man, John, and a Moslem friend.

John takes the Moslem to Mass one Sunday and after the Mass they begin to discuss the meaning of the Eucharist. "Do Catholics really believe that that piece of bread is not bread at all, but Jesus Christ?" the Moslem asked. "We do," said John. "Your Church teaches that the man who was God is really present?" "Yes," says John, "The formula is Body, Blood, and Divinity." "And you believe that?" "Yes," replied John. The Moslem responds, "I don't think you really do believe that. I don't mean to say you are dishonest, but ..." John said, "It is shocking! You don't see how you could ever get down on your knees before that altar?" "No," responded the Moslem student. "I don't see how I could ever get up if I believed that what looks like a little, round piece of bread was really God, Allah himself. I think I would just faint. I would fall at his feet like a dead man."

It takes an unbeliever sometimes to remind us of what we claim to believe. That Moslem student reminds us that if what we say we believe about the Eucharist is true, if we really do believe that Jesus Christ, the God Man is truly present under the veils of bread and wine, then why doesn't our behavior reflect our belief?

My sisters and brothers, over the past few decades, since the great willowing winds of the modern era have blown through the windows of the Church, many of us have lost our grip on a key belief of Catholicism. Jesus Christ is still present in this world. He is not some abstract, distant remote figure out there somewhere in the clouds. No! Jesus IS STILL PRESENT in the concrete reality of the Blessed Sacrament. And from His presence in the Eucharist, Jesus cries out to men and women like you and me, "I want to come and live in your heart." Unfortunately, for too many, Christ has become a remote, but interesting figure, found in the pages of the Bible, sung in the great hymns of the church, but absent from the human heart. But from the sacrament of the altar, Jesus cries out, "I want to come and live in your heart."

In spite of all the calls for reform in the Church, despite the numerous Renew Programs offered in the spirit of Vatican II, true renewal and reform have failed in the lives of many because of the refusal to accept the most basic truth of the Catholic faith... The Christ, who is truly present in the Eucharist, wants to be truly present in your heart and unless we take seriously this truth, we will fail to accept the core of Christ's message.

I read a very sad story the other day. A professor at one of the top Catholic universities in America asked his students the question, "What would you say to God if you died tonight and were asked why you should go to heaven?" Only one in twenty even mentioned Jesus Christ. How would you have answered that question?

The only reason any of us were born, the only reason any of us manages to live another day, the only reason I am not hopeless and hell bound is a person, Jesus Christ, and Him alone.

And He is calling out to you and me today, "I want to come and live in your heart. I no longer want to be an abstract, distant God; I want to be real to you. Do you realize that I will be present at Mass, under the appearance of bread and wine? I want to come and live in your heart."

So many of us come to worship week after week and we walk up the aisle for Communion, hardly stopping to realize what we are doing here. We are receiving the Divine Presence of God Himself, but because we fail to fathom the power of His presence, it has little impact upon our lives. Many leave the church as empty as they came.

Remember the painting of Jesus standing at a door knocking? There is no doorknob on the door on Jesus' side because it is up to you to open that door for Him from the inside.

Far too many of us receive Christ in Communion, but because of our lukewarm faith, we leave Christ standing at the door of our hearts knocking, knocking, and knocking. "Let Me come and live in your heart," He cries.

In the gospel we hear Jesus preaching the words, "Blest are they who hunger and thirst for righteousness, they shall have their fill." To hunger for righteousness is to fall in love with Jesus Christ, to know the strength, the Divine Energy that there is in walking through life with Jesus at you side. There are a whole lot of people who are traveling a lonely road through life, confused, not knowing where they are headed or where they have come from because they have never really opened the door of their heart to God.

I have had my times of darkness, when God seemed so distant and I didn't know where my life was heading; but when I cried out to Jesus and invited Him to once again cross the threshold of my life and live in the home of my heart, then my life began to find meaning again and the light of Jesus filled me with peace.

The Eucharist as Presence

CHAPTER 19

JIM CASTLE AND MOTHER TERESA

Jim Castle was tired the night he boarded his plane in Cincinnati in 1981. To his surprise, walking up the aisle were two nuns clad in simple white habits bordered in blue. Jim realized that his seat companion was going to be Mother Teresa.

Mother Teresa pulled out rosaries – each decade was a different color. Mother Teresa told him the decades represented the various areas of the world. "I pray for the poor and dying on each continent," she said. After the rosary a sense of peace filled him. "Young man," she inquired, "do you pray the rosary often?" "No, not really," he replied. Then she smiled and took his hand... "Well, you will now." She dropped her rosary into his palm. An hour later Jim told his wife, "I feel as if I met a True Sister of God."

A few months later a friend was diagnosed with cancer. Jim gave his rosary from Mother Teresa to her to use. A year later she was cured. Later his sister-in-law fell into a deep depression and Jim loaned her the rosary. "At night I held onto it, just physically held on. I was so lonely and afraid. Yet when I gripped that rosary, I felt as if I held a loving hand." Gradually, she was healed and she returned the rosary. Another friend died peacefully after having the rosary in her hand a few moments.

Is the rosary magic? What is it? Perhaps it is simply this: Each time people came to recognize by holding onto those rosary beads of Mother Teresa, something Mother Teresa knew well: We ALL need a savior, and, if we turn to Him even in simple ways, He will be there for us.

Everyone at some time or another in life is face to face with the stark realization that you can't save yourself. No one can save him or herself, no one can make it through life on his own...he (or she) needs a savior.

There will come a time for each of us when we have to recognize how powerless we are over some things in life. Life's issues are overwhelming sometimes and we can only fall on our knees before the Throne of God and admit, "O God, I need You. I can't handle it on my own." It might be a financial crisis that you find unmanageable. Maybe it is a physical ailment that you can't overcome. Perhaps a relative is dying...and no matter how hard you try to help...you are powerless. Or it might be a personal shortcoming, a terrible habit, a sin that just won't go away, it keeps haunting you. Powerlessness- it is the first step to being saved; recognizing that we cannot do it ourselves. We need a savior who can empower us to make it through the dark times of life. Those are the moments when faith becomes more than a word, and Christian is more than a title; faith in Christ becomes everything. Because He alone is Savior, He alone can give us what we need. He will either shield us or strengthen us. We are helpless without God, without a Savior.

The manager of a ten story building was informed that a man was trapped in an elevator between the second and third floors. He rushed to the grillwork under the stalled car and called to the passenger, "Keep your cool sir, we'll have you out soon. I've phoned for the elevator mechanic." There was a brief pause and a tense voice replied, "I am the elevator mechanic."

We need a real Savior. We can't save ourselves, only Jesus can salvage us from the problems and struggles that often have a death grip on our lives. When we take our faith in Him seriously, we turn to Him for the shelter we need from the problems of life. And, when we find that there is no shelter from our problems, if we have faith in Him, He will strengthen us to carry our burden. I have spoken with people of deep faith who have had to embrace a heavy cross, some overwhelmingly weighty problems, and have done so because they looked to God for that power they themselves couldn't muster to handle the struggle.

Once Pope John XXIII sighed and said, "People have such hard lives...too many problems...so many temptations...such struggles!"

"And you, Holy Father, how do you do it?" asked a friend. "Surely yours must be the hardest life of all. So much responsibility! How do you sleep at night?"

"Oh, I sleep very well," replied Pope John. "Every night, I kneel at the prie-dieu in my room and wash my thoughts and my sins in the blood of Jesus. I see myself dropping them, one by one into the chalice. By dawn, when I rise, I know they are clean. I live in the confidence of the meaning of the Redemption, and it makes me very happy. I get up refreshed every morning, not only from sleep but from the drops of medicine that come only from the Cross." What faith!

My sisters and brothers we have all had our share of trials and struggles and, if we tried to get through them without God's help we probably would end up hardened or bitter from the experience.

A story is told about a young woman who complained about how tough her life had become. She complained to her father one day. He said nothing, but took her to the kitchen and set three pans of water to boiling. To the first pan he added carrots, to the second eggs and to the third ground coffee. After all three had cooked he put their contents into separate bowls and asked his daughter to cut into the eggs and carrots and to smell the coffee. "What does all this mean?" she asked impatiently. "Each food'" he said, "teaches us something about facing adversity, as represented by the boiling water. The carrot went in hard but came out soft and weak. The eggs went in fragile but came out hardened. The coffee however, changed the water to something better. Which will you be like as you face life?" he asked. "Will you give up, become hard, or change troubles into triumph?"

Our God never said He would always shield us from problems and trials, but He did assure us that He would be with us to strengthen us, to bear our burdens with inner peace. But many forget to look to God for their power to be shielded or strengthened and their lives are a mess because of it. There can be no substitutes for Christ as our Savior, our shield and our strength. We live in an age of all kinds of substitutes…margarine subs for butter, Nutra Sweet for sugar, inferior plastics for metal…BUT THERE IS NO SUBSTITUTE FOR CHRIST. He alone can save us. He alone is Savior, our shield and our strength.

Jesus offered one sacrifice for sins and took His seat forever at the right hand of God; now He waits until the enemies are placed beneath His feet. And, what is His greatest enemy, and our greatest enemy? The answer is--anything that leads us to hopelessness and despair. Many face life's problems with no power because they don't realize that Jesus Christ is right there with them-to save them, to shield or strengthen them-no matter how bad it gets.

A mother with many children was telling a friend about her day. Her husband was on a business trip, the washer broke down, it was pouring down rain, the roof was leaking, her children were wild and out of control, everything possible was becoming impossible. She summed up her plight by saying, "I even got a busy signal when I called Dial-A-Prayer."

The message of Jesus is this: "I am a God who is near you. I answer your cries; no matter how often things fall apart, I can pick up the pieces. I am on the line every second, just call." He is Savior. He will either shield you or strengthen you.

A beautiful prayer: I prayed for strength that I might achieve – I was made weak that I might obey. I prayed for health that I might do great things – I was given infirmity that I might do better things. I prayed for riches that I might be happy – I was given poverty that I might be wise. I prayed for power that I might have the praise of men, and was given weakness that I might feel the need of God. I prayed for all things that I might enjoy life, and was given life that I might enjoy all things. I received nothing that I asked for but all that I hoped for my prayers were answered, I am most blessed.

No substitute for Christ. As the old hymn puts it: Blessed assurance Jesus is mine. O what a foretaste of Glory Divine. Heir of salvation, purchase of God, born of His spirit, washed in His blood. This is my story, this is my song, praising my Savior all day long. This is my story, this is my song, praising my Savior all day long.

The Eucharist as Presence

CHAPTER 20

IT'S ELEMENTARY

Sometimes we get so close to the obvious that we become blind. We can't see. Sometimes we miss the meaning of some important spiritual truths because we have become too used to them, too close to them. We have taken them for granted. In the gospel, the disciples are with the Lord on a mountain called Tabor. They saw and heard. In the encounter of Jesus on that mountain it became obvious to them, apparent to them that Jesus was and is God. At every Mass the same encounter occurs for us. Jesus, the divine Son of God, the creator of the universe from whose fingertips tumbled planets, comes to speak His word to us and to draw us up into the mystery of His death on the cross and His resurrection. How obvious is that to you?

I remember being in the Holy Land and traveling to the top of the very mountain spoken of in the gospel, Mount Tabor. I knew this was holy ground I was standing on. In my mind I could see Jesus there, shrouded in light. I could hear God the Father's voice thundering from the skies, "This is my beloved Son, listen to Him." When I came down from the mountain, I felt how blessed I had been to be so close to God and then it occurred to me: I don't need to travel thousands of miles to the Holy Land to encounter God ... it happens every time I come to Mass. God wants to talk to you today, not just in the written words of the scriptures; He wants to talk to your heart.

Many of you have see "The Passion of the Christ" in Aramaic and Latin, two ancient languages used in the time of

Christ. Why use them in the movie? I wondered, and then I concluded that Jesus speaks to our hearts in words that are deeper than what language comes from our mouths. Jesus speaks the language of the heart. How obvious is that to you?

If we listen only with human ears, with hearts closed to the message God wants to bring us today, we'll miss the most important thing God wants to do, touch us in our hearts. In the Mass, we relive the episode in the Bible today. When we present bread and wine at the altar, when we place money in the basket, we are waking up like the apostles did in the gospel, opening our eyes to behold God's presence here. Sometimes we come to mass and our eyes glaze over, our minds miles away. Today, look with eyes of faith at what is happening and listen as Christ speaks to your heart in the language of love. At the most solemn moment of the Mass, when the bells are rung, attention is being called to what is about to happen. Christ once again, through the words of the priest, changes bread into His Body and wine into His Blood. As He did on Mount Tabor, Christ is making his appearance. As the host and chalice are lifted up before our eyes, let the eyes of your faith see the cross lifted up on Calvary. See not bread and wine, but the Savior on the cross crying out to heaven: Father, forgive them; they know not what they do.

Yes, Jesus is praying that the father will forgive us for our failure to comprehend what we are doing at Mass when we do not embrace what is most obvious. The cross of Calvary is planted in our midst so we can encounter the powerful presence of God almighty. As Jesus puts it in scripture: "And when I am lifted up, I will draw all men to myself." How obvious is that to you?

When you come to receive Christ in communion, realize that Christ is accepting you, He is receiving you. He wants to take you into His heart. He wants to embrace you. He wants to console you, strengthen, heal, guide, transform, lift you up and set you free. The awesome presence of God is before our eyes and the meaning of His presence is present to our hearts, but we often miss the obvious truth of what the Mass is.

A story is told of the great Sherlock Holmes and his assistant, Dr. Watson. Holmes was the master of the obvious, commenting,

"Elementary, my dear Watson." when he wanted to point out something which was apparent to him. One night, so the story goes, Watson and Holmes were camping out under the stars. At night, under the stars, Holmes and Watson began to talk. "Watson," said Holmes, "Tell me what you can deduce from what you see as you look at the skies above." "Well," said Watson, "the moon is full." "Yes," said Holmes, "what else." "The stars are shining brightly in their constellations," "Yes, yes, what else?" "It might rain tomorrow given the cloud cover to the west," "Yes, yes, yes, what else?" "I don't know." "Elementary, my dear Watson, someone stole our tent."

The obvious is important! We often miss the obvious. The Mass is an encounter with the living God. It's elementary!

The Eucharist as Presence

CHAPTER 21

CHRIST'S KEYS TO REAL HAPPINESS

A newspaper article entitled, "Snowbound Dying Couple Leave Diary" offered me some food for spiritual thought. This couple ventured out on a 60-mile trip through the mountains, when their car skidded into a snow bank. They were found two months later. The couple had left a diary, written by the light of their glove compartment. The diary goes on to explain how the couple occupied themselves by singing hymns, taking catnaps and quoting Bible verses. She also wrote how they ate Rolaids, a stick of gum and two teaspoon sized packets of jelly and would scrape frost off the windows to drink. They had left a last testament to whoever would listen. They wrote, "So many things I want to say. I want you all to enjoy your life and remember what is so dreadful today will be forgotten next year. Please be a family. A drink of water for me will never go unappreciated again and a bite of food, any kind."

On the feast day of the Solemnity of Corpus Christi, the Body of Christ, we listen to another last testament, the last testament of Jesus Christ. In fact, we listen to it at every Mass, but perhaps today we can put on a new set of ears and hear its beauty with a new enthusiasm. In the book of Hebrews we read, Christ is the mediator of a new covenant so that those who are called may receive the promised eternal inheritance. The Lord has left us a great inheritance and at every Mass the last will and testament of Jesus Christ is read once again. We have a great inheritance left us by one who made a fortune and wants to leave it to us and the inheritance is not some diminishable sum which perishes with the passing of time. No, the inheritance we have been left is an eternal crown, an imperishable treasure.

The inheritance is this; we have been left three golden keys of happiness. These three keys to happiness can be described this way: fret not, faint not, fear not. Fret not, God loves you; faint not, God holds you; fear not; God keeps you. This is Christ's parting gift to us. These are the three gifts of happiness which are part of that imperishable treasure given thanks for at every Mass. When Christ gives us His Body under the appearance of simple bread and His Blood under the appearance of fine wine, it is not the body and blood of a dead man. No, it is the life-giving energy of God Himself. A power and energy is transferred to us in communion so that we may begin to realize the great testament Christ has left us. When He gives us His Body and Blood, He gives us those keys of happiness. Once again: this is my Body, fret not, I love you; this is my Body and Blood, faint not, I hold you; this is my Body broken and my Blood poured out, fear not, I keep you.

When on this feast, the Blessed Eucharist is taken outside and a procession is formed to carry the Lord's Body and Blood for public adoration, we are reminding ourselves and the world. Here in Jesus Christ's Body and Blood we find the three keys to eternal happiness. Here world, look – look. Here in Jesus in the Eucharist we find the keys to eternal serenity and peace. Here world, in Christ is your salvation. Don't look to drugs, don't look to violence, and don't look to money or sex for your happiness. Look here. Jesus Christ is the Bread of Life. He has left us a great inheritance--the three golden keys of happiness. Listen O neighborhood filled with violence, drugs, degradation and darkness. Christ is offering his keys to happiness: fret not, God loves you; faint not, God holds you; fear not, God keeps you.

On July 17, 1938 a pilot by the name of Corrigan left New York's Bennett Field in an attempt to fly non-stop from New York to Los Angeles. Corrigan reads the wrong end of his compass needle and without a radio or navigational equipment, lands 28 hours and 3,150 miles later in Dublin, Ireland.

Have you checked your compass today to see if you are headed in the right direction? Look to Christ in the Eucharist. It is no dead man's body and blood here, but the life-giving, energizing, power-packed source of divine life. Here at Mass, Christ's last testament is proclaimed and again here are Christ's keys to real happiness.

The Eucharist as Presence

CHAPTER 22

HELP AND HOPE

Thirty-five million people are popping Prozac these days according to a "U.S. News and World Report" article. Depression is increasing in spite of Prozac and other popular feel-good pills. By 2020, some observers say, depression will be the world's second most disabling disease, after heart disease.

A growing sense of helplessness and hopelessness is among men and women today. In spite of technological advances, that most basic issue which faces every one of us, surfaces and finds no lasting answer in the annals of medical science. Science can only begin to scratch the surface in the search for a solution to everyone's hunger for hope. The Eucharist, the Blessed Sacrament, is the focus of the Corpus Christi feast because the Church wants us to remember where hope and help can be found to feed the hunger that grips the lives of so many today. You may say, "Well I'm not depressed, hopeless or helpless." You need not be depressed. You need not be plagued by feelings of hopelessness to recognize one all important truth: Nothing is going to give me lasting peace, but God.

Statistics bear this truth out. David Larson, psychiatrist, writes in "Christianity Today" magazine that 19 out of 20 studies confirm that religion plays a positive role in preventing alcoholism. Sixteen out of 17 studies show a positive role in reducing suicide. Religious commitment was associated with lower rates of mental disorder, drug use, and premarital sex. People who attend Church regularly even show much lower blood pressure levels. In short, what all this points to is Christ, who is the source of peace for the troubled soul and everyone is troubled.

And where can I meet this Christ in order for Him to feed the hunger for peace in my soul? Where can I locate this God who promises me the strength I need? Where can I contact this Jesus who promises me hope, an enduring strength that goes beyond the Prozac? How can I make an appointment with a psychiatrist who treats me free of charge and pays the bill himself by His Body and Blood, crucified and shed on the cross?

THERE, THERE, THERE—in the Most Blessed Sacrament. You need not look far. He is there. Jesus is the psychiatrist who can heal your deepest wounds. The Lord takes walk-ins. No appointment necessary. In the Mass, at the altar, you can find the food that will rid your heart of its aching hunger for peace. Here He is. His name is Jesus and He is present at the altar in a few moments under the humble appearances of bread and wine. He is now present in this tabernacle, in every tabernacle in every Catholic Church in the world.

"This is my Body" He says again over the bread, using my mouth to speak His words. "This is my Blood," the Divine Healer says over the wine, using my hands to hold the cup of salvation, yours and mine. Do you believe He is in the Blessed Sacrament? Do you really believe in the power of God present in the Blessed Sacrament? Interestingly, studies show that people who believe in Christianity but do not practice it experience greater stress. People who claim to believe in God, but who neglect to live their faith have higher rates of anxiety than the general population. Perhaps there is so much emotional upheaval in society today because so many so called Christians, Catholics included, in the presence of Christ in the Blessed Sacrament, claim to believe, but it doesn't go beyond lip service. We are so foolish, so many. Christ is the solution to life's problems. The remedy for what ails the soul.

And He is here in the Eucharist. Only a fool will imperil his life by professing faith with the lips, but denying belief in the heart.

St. Anthony of Padua, (d. 1231) was involved in a most dramatic miracle of the Eucharist. It also involved, of all things, a mule. The history of the saint relates that a man named Boniville, believed to have been an Albigensian heretic, who rejected the validity of all the Sacraments, was one day in Toulouse questioning the saint about the Sacrament of the Altar. Boniville denied the real presence of Jesus Christ in the consecrated Host while the saint steadfastly affirmed it. As a test, one or the other suggested that the choice be made by Boniville's mule. Both men agreed. The mule was kept in its stall for three days, and deprived of food during all that time. At the end of the fast, a great crowd of both believers and unbelievers assembled to witness the proceedings. When the mule was brought before St. Anthony, he held a consecrated Host before the animal, while Boniville attempted to feed it oats and hay. The mule took no notice of the food, but fell to its knees before the Blessed Sacrament. The Catholics who witnessed the miracle expressed unbounded joy, while the unbelievers were thoroughly confused. Boniville is said to have been subsequently converted, together with a great number of the heretics.

A dumb donkey recognized what we fail to see, Christ is present in the Blessed Sacrament. An ass humbled itself in adoration before the Blessed Sacrament because it could see what so many, so called intelligent eyes, refuse to see. In the Blessed Sacrament is your God, who comes to feed our souls. Here is Jesus, our only hope. Adore Him, bow before Him. We must be wiser than a dumb donkey. We think we are so smart, but an ass knows better.

Yes, sometimes Prozac or mood lifting drug therapy may be necessary. Sometimes a psychiatrist must be sought, but in the final analysis you and I must admit the limitedness, the limitations of the human and the medical, the imperfections of man in dealing with ultimate questions, such as hope, hopelessness, life and death, peace and disharmony, joy and despair. Christ is the ultimate solution and He is present in the Eucharist.

Renew your faith during the next Mass you attend. When you participate in a Eucharistic procession, when we take the Blessed Sacrament and form a procession, profess your faith. By means of a public Eucharistic procession we give public witness and testimony to our faith as if we were crying out to the whole world: "THERE, THERE, THERE in the Blessed Sacrament. There is Jesus, the Savior of the world, the hope, the strength, the peace, that every heart longs for-- adore Him."

The Eucharist as Presence

CHAPTER 23

FAITH, LOVE AND PEACE

An artist wanted to paint the most beautiful picture in the world and so he asked a clergyman, "What is the most beautiful thing in the world?" "Faith," answered the clergyman, "You can feel it in every Church, and find it at any altar." He asked a bride the same question, "What is the most beautiful thing in the world?" "Love, love builds poverty into riches, sweetens tears, makes much of little. Without it, there is no beauty." A soldier gave this reply, "Peace is the most beautiful thing in the world. War is the most ugly. Where you find peace, you find beauty." Faith, love and peace--how can I paint them wondered the artist. Returning home, he found faith in the eyes of his children, love in the eyes of his wife and there in his home was the peace that faith and love built. So he painted the most beautiful thing in the world and when he finished it, he called it "home".

A homecoming of sorts occurs at every Mass, for when you come before the altar to receive your King in communion, you are being transported to that dimension where you and Christ are totally at peace and in love. Communion takes us home. It is a foretaste of our heavenly home. We reflect with joy upon the mighty mystery of Christ's presence in the Eucharist. The feast reminds us of the words of Jesus, "I am with you always, until the end of time. Take – eat. Take – drink. This is my Body and Blood." And it is upon this mysterious presence of Christ that we are reflecting when we talk about the Eucharist as going home.

Modern men and women are people with addresses, but never home. They search frantically for peace, for serenity, for consolation, for strength, for love, like enduring a long trek on a ceaseless treadmill. Modern men and women get nowhere in the search for peace in the heart because they are looking in the wrong places. Many are like people with addresses, but never home because they are empty on the inside. Neither booze, nor drugs, nor sex, nor power, nor popularity, nor money, nor clothes, nor jewelry, nor food, nor a car can make your life or mine what God designed it to be. It is here (in the heart), not out there where we find what we really need. Within us is a house of love that human hands alone cannot build. In here God wants to take up residence to fill the emptiness.

No matter what we accomplish in this life, there is deep within each of us an empty sensation. Like a house once occupied and now abandoned, our heart is in need of an occupant. The Eucharist we celebrate and receive is a principal way for us to get in touch with the home within us. The Eucharist, Holy Communion, reminds us that only God can satisfy the hungering heart. Only Christ can fill the empty rooms within. Only Jesus can make us feel at home with ourselves and with each other.

We often think in the ways of the world. I am what I drive, I am what I wear, and I am what I live in. But we are what we eat, as Christians, because when we eat the Eucharist we become occupied territory — family people, people whose hearts are occupied by Christ.

St. Anthony parish in Des Moines is my home parish. There is a very old tradition which my people still observe at St. Anthony's, a procession of the Blessed Sacrament throughout the neighborhoods and around the Church. The Blessed Sacrament is carried in solemn procession accompanied by hundreds of people carrying colorful banners and singing hymns of praise. This is public witness to their faith in the Eucharist, but the custom underscores the point of the feast of Corpus Christi. Christ walks with us along the highways and by-ways of live. Christ is not just out there somewhere, but Christ wants to be walking within us, occupying that dwelling place inside us, where our heart beats, where love resides. As this Eucharistic bread is processed through the streets of our old neighborhood, we are reminded Christ wants to dwell within. He has given Himself as food. He wants to take up residence inside us.

Some time ago, divers discovered a 400 year old Spanish ship buried in water off the coast of Northern Ireland. Among the treasures found in the ship was a man's gold wedding ring. Etched into the wide band of the ring was a hand holding a heart with these words, "I have nothing more to give you."

The same image and words could be used to describe what Christ is saying to you and me today. I have nothing more to give you. I have given you my very self. I have sacrificed my life for you on the wood of the cross. I have offered my love to you under the appearances of bread and wine. I want to dwell within you. I want to reside within the home of your heart. I have nothing more to give you.

In the gospel story the disciples are sent to prepare a room for the Passover Supper. They find an upstairs room, spacious, furnished and in order. That was the place they were to get ready for the Last Supper. Look within the home of your life now and see the room you are to prepare for this banquet feast we call the Mass. That space within you is where Christ wants to come and dwell. An old saying puts it, "I sought to hear the voice of God, climb the highest steeple, but God declared, 'Down, down again, I dwell with my people.'"

A painter once wanted to paint the most beautiful picture in the world and so he painted a portrait and called it "home". But remember, that home within us is a house with an address, but empty on the inside unless Christ comes to occupy its rooms. Come, O bread of life. Come O Christ our King. Come and dwell within me. Nothing can take up the space in my heart. Nothing can give life, but You. All else will evaporate, corrode, mold, or decay. You alone are eternal. You alone can satisfy my hungry heart. Be the occupant of my home within. Amen.

The Eucharist as Presence

CHAPTER 24

SO GREAT A SACRAMENT

"Humbly let us voice our homage for so great a sacrament" (Hymn of St. Thomas Aquinas, 1250). One of the greatest traditions of the Italian people in America is the spaghetti dinner every Sunday afternoon. It is an opportunity for the family to get together for what we would consider the major meal of the week--an occasion to share a common meal and the things that are happening in each other's lives and a means for building up the bonds of love and brotherhood that a family ideally shares.

What happens at a Sunday meal such as the one I have described is in the real way, analogous or similar, to what happens at the Eucharist, the Mass. Not exactly the same, Mass is not a common meal, but similar. It is no accident that Jesus chose a meal as a means to share Himself with us and to be present with us after His ascension. A meal has power packed meaning. When we love someone, we take them out for dinner. There are very few marriages, I am sure, that did not begin with a date in which the couple went out to dinner. Why is the meal so powerful? Because a meal has the power to express common bonds and has the power to build-up relationships between people. We become one in the one meal that we share.

In Corinthians, St. Paul says, "As the loaf of bread is one, we, many though we are, are one body for we all partake of one loaf." For a meal, a group of people gather and share one food. Through eating the meal together, the group becomes a unity, like one happy family. After a dinner date, if the couple lets the meaning of the meal take effect, the couple has grown into an oneness, a deeper appreciation for each other--so also at the Mass. Many that we are, we share one common meal. If we let the meaning of this meal take effect, we will grow into a oneness with each other. We will become a family of faith.

The Mass is no common meal though. Again, this meal, the Mass, is sacred for we share in the Lord Himself in a very special and unique way. The food we eat at Mass has a deeper meaning and impact for through this sacramental bread, God becomes intimately present to us. St. Cyril of Alexandria compared this union to two pieces of wax melted together. St. Theresa of Lisieux, the Little Flower, described her First Communion as a fusion with Christ, a melting together. He becomes present to us not as a God, who is out there, but He is present to us as a God who is willing to share Himself with us by giving Himself in the meal itself. As we take each bread into our body, Jesus sacramentally enters into the heart of our lives, we become part of Him as He becomes part of us.

As the gospel says, "Jesus is the living Bread come down from heaven." This meal is more powerful and says much more than an ordinary spaghetti dinner. The Mass says that we are a community of people convinced of the importance of Jesus in our lives.

Picture a child running to meet his father. He throws his little arms around his father's neck, hugging him with all his might. But the father sweeps the child up in his big, strong arms, hugging him even more lovingly. Communion is something like that. We embrace Jesus. We take Him into our hearts. Jesus embraces us. He takes us into His heart. Think of this and you will begin to realize that it is not our love, our longings, our prayers which are important, although they should be there. Most important is the limitless love of Christ--His longing to embrace us, to share His life with us. He wants us to remain in Him, just as we want Him to remain in us.

The Mass says that we are serious about being Christians, being members of the Body of Christ, believers, and members of the Church. The Mass says that we are serious about loving God and loving others for love of Him. The Eucharist, unlike an ordinary meal, expresses these truths, love of God, love of neighbor, truths of our faith.

Let us ask ourselves what the Mass and receiving Holy Communion mean to us. Does the receiving of Jesus in Holy Communion express our love for Him as He is master of our lives? Does the reception of Holy Communion express our love for others? Two words which describe the Eucharist are opportunity and openness. Opportunity to deepen ties, openness to God who binds us. If the Mass does not express these facts of our lives, love of God and love of neighbor, then much work needs to be done. If we do not live as if Jesus makes a difference, what meaning is Communion? The Eucharist gives us the strength to work towards this, but we show that Jesus makes a difference by loving our fellow man daily. This meal, the Mass, has power packed meaning if we let God work in our lives. Let our prayer today be, O Sacrament most holy, O Sacrament divine, All praise and all thanksgiving be every moment Thine. Amen.

Section Three

The Eucharist As Communion

The Eucharist as Communion

CHAPTER 25

THE MASS, WHAT'S HAPPENING?

"We cannot choose our family, our relatives or our neighbors, but we are," as Emerson says, "the architects of our own friendships."

While the disciples made their way along the road to the village named Emmaus, Jesus approached and began to walk along with them. What a beautiful image of the Christian life! Jesus walks along with us through the highways and by-ways of life. He is our most intimate companion.

The word "companion" is rich and fraught with meaning. Two Latin words, cum and panis - with and bread. A companion is one with whom we share bread. In ancient times when you invited someone to break bread with you, it was an invitation to friendship. That invitation to companionship with Jesus is extended to us at every Mass. Jesus wants to walk with us through life and he wants to be our guide so that we may fulfill His plan for our lives. God wants to lead us along the sure and safe path which leads us to heaven. Where are you headed in your life?

There's a story of a reverend frustrated with sleepers during his sermons. He decided after many weeks of a man sleeping during his sermon to teach him a lesson. When the man fell asleep the minister instructed the congregation to remain seated no-matter what. Then he said softly, "Now everyone who is going to hell, stand up." Then the sleeper woke up and jumped up out of his seat. The minister smiled knowingly and everyone in the congregation watched. The sleeper, now awake, looked around quizzically and quipped, "Reverend, I don't know where we're going, but it looks like you and I are the only two going there."

Are you going where Jesus is leading you? At every Mass we receive our marching orders from the Master and at Mass we pledge anew to walk with our companion, Jesus, and never leave His side because He never leaves ours.

I want to look at the Mass to learn how the Mass teaches us where we're going and how to get there.

When Mass begins a procession comes down the aisle led by the cross. This reminds us that we are travelers and Jesus is leading us along the road to heaven. We are led to the altar where we will break bread, where we will share the Divine Supper with our Divine Companion. We confess our sins as we cry out, "Lord have mercy, Christ have mercy." We admit to Jesus that we have detoured along the road leading to heaven and we are sorry.

The first main part of the mass is called the Liturgy of the Word. Here we listen to the Master companion, Jesus, give us instructions for our journey through life. If we are good listeners, we will listen to the instructions for our journey through life and learn how to stay on the right road. The inspired, anointed Word of God is proclaimed. The very words from the lips of Jesus are spoken again. They are a now word, a today word, a word which must penetrate our minds and hearts. We have to sit still awhile and listen so that we won't act on impulse and dash off in the wrong direction.

A story is told of a knight who returned to his castle at evening. He was a mess. His armor was dented, his helmet out of shape, his face bloody and his horse was limping. The lord of the castle asked, "What has befallen you, sir knight?" The knight answered, "O sire, I have been laboring in your service, fighting and harassing your enemies to the west." "You've been what?" cried the king. "But I don't have any enemies to the west." "Oh," said the knight. "Well, I think you do now." If we listen to our marching orders given at Mass, we won't be fighting the wrong enemy in the wrong place.

The second part of the Mass is called The Liturgy of the Eucharist. Here the Lord Jesus sits at the table as He did with the disciples on the road to Emmaus. Here He reveals Himself in the breaking of the bread. But this bread is no mere bread and Jesus is no ordinary companion with whom we eat this banquet. No, what looks like bread and wine are really the very body, blood, soul and divinity of Jesus Himself.

At the altar, Jesus shows us His wounds in His hands. Here He tells us, "Look and see how big the price I paid for you so that you may live forever with me in heaven. Eat and drink. This food and drink are a pledge of my presence with you along this road of life…walk with me." And when we receive Communion we pledge our commitment to Jesus. Jesus, I shall walk with you…I am yours. I am with you as you travel over the hills and through the valleys of life. Jesus, I shall walk with you. Let nothing separate me from you again.

And then, at the end of Mass, the procession once again forms and heads out. Led by the Cross of Jesus we go forward into the world to march where He marches, to where He leads and to do what He asks of us.

What a better world this would be if we realized what happens at Mass. Jesus, our Divine Companion, dines with us and gives us His marching orders for the day and for the week. Here at mass time and space are bridged and we stand on Calvary with the Crucified Savior. Here, on Calvary, at the Mass, we begin the message, "Come Follow Me."

The beautiful hymn, "What a Friend We Have in Jesus", reminds me of the companionship and intimacy we share at Mass with the Savior and the companionship we share with Him along the road of life.

What a friend we have in Jesus. All our sins and grieves to bear, what a privilege to carry everything to God in prayer. O what peace we often forfeit, O what needless pain we bear, all because we do not carry everything to God in prayer. Have we trials and temptations? Is there trouble anywhere? We should never be discouraged. Take it to the Lord in prayer. Can we find a friend so faithful? Who will all our sorrows share?

The Eucharist as Communion

CHAPTER 26

DOOMSDAY CLOCK

Atomic scientists have what is referred to as the Doomsday Clock. On November 26, 1991, atomic scientists set back the hands of their Doomsday Clock to 11:43, the farthest it has ever been from midnight. The clock depicts their estimate of humanities proximity to nuclear annihilation. The closest it had come to signaling doomsday was in 1953, after the U.S. tested the hydrogen bomb. Its hands then stood at 11:58.

That clock does not reflect God's clock, however. His clock's hands are not moved by arms treaties or the decline of communism. His clock continues to tick, tick, tick. The hands of His clock are moved by His mercy.

We, as individuals and the world as a whole will one day be judged by God who holds this universe in His hands and, from whose fingertips, tumbled planets and galaxies at creation. Yes, judgment, as we say in the creed; and He will come to judge the living and the dead. But one thing must be forever held tightly in mind. God came into this world so that we find the way to pass the judgment and live with Him forever in heaven. He is a judge who wants to grant us eternal joy - not eternal pain, but the choice is ours.

I don't think we realize the part we play in our own judgment and how we can influence our own destiny, moving the hands of the Doomsday Clock backwards instead of forward towards annihilation.

When I think of how a person can influence his destiny and the destiny of others, I think of Bill Wilson. Bill Wilson founded Alcoholic Anonymous.

Since the founding of Alcoholic Anonymous in the 30's to this day, millions have benefited from the simple message taught by Wilson's AA (Alcoholic Anonymous) program. Today, approximately 15 million persons are actively involved in 500,000 recovery groups, which are based on Wilson's simple 12 steps to recovery. His simple contribution to this world has set back the personal Doomsday Clock of many people, due to the emphasis his program places upon dependence and guidance from a higher power and the complete deflation of false pride.

Holy Thursday is a day to reflect upon our own Doomsday Clock. Every time we celebrate the Eucharist, we set the Doomsday Clock back, because the Eucharist empowers our lives to depend on God and to break the back of pride and arrogance. It is pride and arrogance which have led, and still lead humanity on the pathway to destruction. On the first Holy Thursday, Christ gave us the Eucharist as an antidote for the poison of pride.

Chuck Colson was one of the key ringleaders of the Watergate conspiracy and he spent a number of years in prison as a consequence. He was one of the most ruthless and obstinate of all the co-conspirators.

While in prison, Colson did a lot of reading. Once he read a book called, "Mere Christianity" by C.S. Lewis. The following words pierced his heart like a hot knife through butter: "Pride leads to every other vice. It is the complete Anti God state of mind. As long as you are proud, you cannot know God. A proud man is always looking down on things. As long as you are looking down, you cannot see anything above you." Colson said he felt naked and unclean as he sat there in his prison cell, and suddenly he confessed his sin of pride and how it led him into darkness. He turned his life over to God and was reborn that fateful day in the darkness of a prison cell. Now he knows what living in the light of love is all about and his life is becoming a sacrifice of love as he goes about the country preaching for Christ. When the Lord said, "Do this in memory of me," He means begin to leave pride behind and live for Me.

My sisters and brothers, there is a judgment on this world, and upon us, because our world is so steeped in the darkness of pride - a pride which paralyzes us from doing or seeing anything above us because we always look down on everything and everyone around us, and this paralysis of pride moves this world, minute by minute, closer to annihilation - death by suicide.

Holy Thursday is a summons to you and me - Come, kneel before the Lord and confess your pridefulness. Come, kneel in humility, as Christ knelt and washed the feet of his disciples. Come, celebrate the Eucharist and commit yourself to making your life a sacrifice of love for others.

There is a twofold meaning to the words, "This is my Body, This is my Blood." Christ's words of self-giving, but also ours. For, when we join our words to Christ's we break out of the paralysis of pride and live for God and for love.

William Booth founded the Salvation Army, an organization which puts love into action. Someone asked Booth the secret of his success. With tear filled eyes he said, "There have been men with greater brains or opportunities than I, but I made up my mind that God would have all of William Booth there was." Several years after, when General Booth's daughter heard about her father's comment regarding his full surrender to God, she said, "That was not really his secret. His secret was that he never took it back."

The Eucharist is an act of self surrender to God. Every time we celebrate it with understanding, placing ourselves on the altar too, the Doomsday Clock is set back. But the secret to keeping that Doomsday Clock moving backwards is, like William Booth, never to take our life back from God.

I offer myself to you. To build with me and to do with me as you will. Relieve me of the bondage of pride, that I may better do your will. Take away my difficulties that victory may then bear witness to those I would help of Thy power, Thy Love and Thy way of life. May I do your will always.

A PRIEST'S PRAYER FOR HOLY THURSDAY, 1996

O God ever-present, ever-powerful, ever-merciful. As we gather in the upper room, with your Divine Son, we pause to consider the gift of priesthood. On this night, your son commissioned the twelve, and every other priest, to do what He did - to celebrate the Eucharist until He comes again in glory.

The twelve were clearly weak men and so is every priest who follows in their footsteps. The only source of strength for those weak, inconsistent and sinful apostles was the power of the Holy Spirit and so too for us. So anoint every priest again tonight with the power of the Holy Spirit. In spite of our weaknesses, strengthen your people. In spite of our inconsistency, make your people constant in their love for you. In spite of our sins, make us channels of holiness. Thank you Lord, for calling me and every other priest by name. May my life be a sacrifice of praise to you, O Father, ever glorious and ever true. Amen.

The Eucharist as Communion

CHAPTER 27

MY HEART IS WITH YOURS

In 1549, Christianity was flourishing in Japan. St. Francis Xavier had missionized the country and the faith was spreading all over Japan. But the shogun, the Emperor of Japan, turned against the adherents of the new faith and began a fierce persecution of Christians. Thousands faced cruel torture and death. Christians had their ears cut off and were driven through the streets in ox carts to warn others of the dangers of being Christian. After the wholesale slaughter of thousands of Christians, the true faith was all but blotted out in Japan for the next three hundred years.

Missionaries returned to Japan in the 1860's and they fully expected to find no trace of the Christian religion since it had been blotted out three hundred years prior. To their surprise, the missionaries discovered that the faith had, in fact, survived in secret for almost three centuries. The church had gone underground. The secret password among the underground Christians to identify one another was the words: My heart is with your heart. Those beautiful words summarize what Holy Thursday is all about - My heart is with your heart. If faith means anything, it means being of one heart. That oneness of heart can only come about when we share in a similar experience.

The disciples were of one mind and one heart the scripture tells us. Why? They were one because they had all experienced the power and the person of Jesus. The disciples had spent time with Jesus. They had listened to Him, they had eaten with Him, they had witnessed His miracles and they all witnessed His resurrected Presence. And, because of that experience, they were able to give their lives in service to the cause of Christ. And most of them shed their blood like the Japanese martyrs did, because the experience of Jesus was so powerful and the love they bore for Him in their hearts so real, that it could sustain them, even unto the sufferings and pain or martyrdom. How powerful has been our experience of Christ? Has it touched our hearts?

Author Leonard Griffith tells the story of a young Korean exchange student who was a leader in Christian circles at the University of Pennsylvania. One evening in 1958, the foreign exchange student left his apartment to mail a letter. As he returned from the mailbox, he was met by eleven, leather jacketed teens. Without a word, they beat him with a black jack, a lead pipe and their shoes and fists and left him lying dead in the gutter. All of Philadelphia sired out for vengeance. The district attorney planned to seek the death penalty for the arrested youth, and then, this letter arrived signed by the boy's parents and twenty other relatives in Korea:

Our family has met together and we have decided to petition that the most generous treatment possible within the laws of your government be given to those who have committed this criminal action. In order to give evidence of our sincere hope contained in this petition, we have decided to save money to start a fund to be used for the religious, educational, vocational and social guidance for the boys when they are released. We have dared to express our hope with a spirit received from the gospel of our Savior Jesus Christ who died for our sins.

Their hearts were one with the merciful heart of Jesus, and, this attitude of mercy and love came about because they had experienced the power and the person of Jesus. When you meet Jesus in a significant way, he changes your heart.

On the First Holy Thursday, Jesus met with His twelve, and there He took simple bread and wine and said, "This is my Body, This is my Blood shed for you. Do This in Remembrance of Me." But this remembering goes beyond the gathering at Mass. It means remembering Jesus in acts of love and mercy when we leave the church. When we love with the heart of Jesus, we are living the Mass.

When we come together to celebrate Mass we are being empowered by Jesus' Spirit to go out and take His heart to the world. The world needs the heart of Jesus more than ever. In the world there is so much hatred, so much loneliness, so much violence. And Jesus says, "May your heart be with my heart. Touch the world."

At every mass when we hear the words, "Do This in Remembrance of Me." Let those words strike your heart - piercing it as surely as the lance pierced the heart of Jesus on the cross. Let the words open a gaping wound so that your heart and Jesus may be one.

Someone once described the union of the Christian with Christ at Mass this way: When two candles are placed side by side, touching each other, eventually the two become fused as one - one light ... one flame. So may our hearts become one with Christ.

Because, at every Mass, we come up next to the Savior, our heart touching His heart ... One flame touching another. In time, may those flames become one.

When the Japanese who formed the Christian underground met, they signaled their Christian identity by saying, "My heart is with your Heart." May my heart and yours by with Jesus' heart first, last and always.

A PRIEST'S PRAYER FOR HOLY THURSDAY, 2002

"I will take the cup of salvation and call upon the name of the Lord. Praising, I will call upon the Lord, and I will be saved from my enemies."

On this holy night, O Savior Christ, we call upon your holy name. Your name is holy and the holiness you offer us this night can transform our lives. Our world needs transformation. In the spirit of the first apostles, we have abandoned, betrayed and denied you countless times. Sin grips our hearts and we cry to you, "Save me O Lord from my enemies, as I call upon your name." As we take up the Cup of Salvation, we ask for the strength to convert our hearts, to renew the church and transform lives.

So many priests stand before your altar this night, in churches throughout the world, leading their people as they share the Food of Salvation. Dispel the dark cloud of suspicion and fear over your church. Restore within your church, the spirit of holiness in priests and people. On this night I pledge myself anew, renewing the pledge I made so many years ago: YOURS I AM, YOURS I HAVE ALWAYS BEEN AND YOURS I FOREVER WISH TO BE. AMEN.

The Eucharist as Communion

CHAPTER 28

I STOOD WITH PETER

Late one summer night, almost twenty years ago, the sleep of a dormitory of graduate students and their professors was dramatically interrupted by the blare of a fire alarm. Confused and blurry eyed, the residents stumbled out into the thick July night. There was no fire - just a drill. Both professors and students thought it was the real thing, so they were all loaded down with books, notes and other valuables that they wanted to save from incineration. However, one of the professors who stood pajama clad in the college courtyard, and, who had long been working on an important research project, carried nothing but a shabby umbrella (a very old gift from his parents long ago). The umbrella was slung casually over his shoulder. One of his colleagues approached him, and, with a face willed with consternation, asked him why he had saved an umbrella and not his research notes. The professor looked surprised at first, but then, unfurling the umbrella, he answered simply, "This I treasure." It suddenly began to rain.

Like the wise old professor, we too are challenged on Holy Thursday night. The question is posed, "What do you treasure?"

On the First Holy Thursday, the treasures of many hearts were laid bare. For Judas, the great treasure was money. He sold out His Savior for thirty pieces of silver. For Peter, the great treasure was safety and self preservation. He denied the Messiah three times in one evening, because he knew to have recognized Christ would have meant his own arrest. It was too costly a price to pay.

For the chief priest of the temple who had Jesus arrested, his heart's treasure was the preservation of his precious position as chief priest. To have any competitor around Jesus was too threatening. "Let's get rid of the competition," he concluded. For the guards who arrested Jesus, duty was paramount. No matter if the one they were apprehending was innocent. Their orders were clear ... Arrest Him.

On Holy Thursday, the treasure of our heart is laid bare too. Do we have the nerve to take a look? Most of us boldly claim that if we had been there that first night in the garden, we would have defended the Savior. No one would have laid a foul hand on Him with me around. Is that so? Like Peter, our words are bold, but our deeds are few. We are proud people.

When Jesus wanted to wash Peter's feet, he protested, "You shall never wash my feet." But a few hours later this strong man broke under the pressure and ran for cover, frightened to tears. He wouldn't let Christ lay a hand on him to wash his feet, but he let a mob lay hundreds of violent hands on the one he claimed was His Lord. Come on Peter. Who are you kidding? Words are cheap! Like Peter, we can kid no one, really.

We claim no one would lay a violent hand on Jesus if we were there, and yet, the Lord is taken by violence every time we cut and run when the Christian Life demands anything from us beyond the easy and simple requirements.

Christ, taken in violence every time we ignore His Commandments and turn a deaf ear. The world might reject me if I take my Christianity too seriously. Christ is scourged and we stand by passively watching when the lonely are left abandoned, the sick are left unattended, the old rejected and shuttled off to a rest home far away. We leave Christ to be taken by force when our faith is no better than a badge we wear, not a life we live.

How great a treasure is your Christ? "Come on Peter, who are you kidding? How much do you really care for this Christ?" We are Peter, too.

And, soon after that First Holy Thursday, the hearts that betrayed God were busted open. And Judas couldn't bear what he saw in that busted heart of his; he killed himself. The high priest became flushed with rage when confronted with the one he had falsely arrested. He tore his garments in rage, his heart was torn in shame. But Peter looked at his guilt ridden, busted heart, and, filled with tears, his heart was washed clean, and Peter was reborn. Only when Peter was humbled in desperation over his denial of Christ was he able to let Christ truly wash, not just his feet, but the deepest recesses of his hardened heart. The defenses built to keep God from getting too close were broken down and God's Love flushed his heart clean with the fresh water of His Mercy.

Let Christ wash not your feet, but your heart. Look at your life. What have you really treasured? Admit it, you have denied your God and turned Him countless times over to the violent hands of those who would try to destroy Him again. I have denied Him whenever indifference towards other's needs kept me from reaching out my hands to help--and when my faith took back seat to my pleasure, my comforts and my desires.

When Christ takes Bread and breaks it, he says, "This is my Body given up for you." He is reminding us: I was given over to die a horrible death, because of you and others who refused to pay the price and defend me.

When He says, "This cup is my Blood shed for you." He is challenging us to look at the facts. We cut and run every time our faith may require a little pain or sacrifice on our part. He shed His blood because we refused to lift a little finger to live our faith. What do you treasure?

Holy Thursday is the night of Christ's arrest, the night of His washing His disciples' feet, the night when He gave us the Mass as an everlasting memorial of His Love. And on Holy Thursday night we confess: Yes, I stood with Peter that First Holy Thursday. I cut and ran when the going got tough. I was too proud to let my God lay a hand on me and wash my feet, but not strong enough to defend my Master from having violent hands laid on Him. I, like Peter, need the Body and the Blood of the Savior, so that my heart might be flushed clean, and my God may become my heart's truest treasure.

A PRIEST'S PRAYER FOR HOLY THURSDAY, 1985

O Divine Son of God, I kneel before you again, on this the anniversary of that night, when, nearly 2000 years ago, you instituted the Sacrament of the Priesthood. Today, priests throughout the world celebrate that great event. Tonight, throughout the world, your priests stand again before your altar to celebrate with their people, the Divine Mysteries of your dying and rising.

Tonight I renew before you and your people, my commitment to you and to your priesthood. Make me faithful, make my ministry fruitful. Use me as your instrument in your service. Only do not forsake me, for if I am left to myself, I shall surely bring it all to destruction. Lord, I am yours. Amen.

The Eucharist as Communion

CHAPTER 29

REMEMBER THE ALAMO

Remember the Alamo? A few days before the final siege of the Alamo, Colonel William Barret Travis faced the 232 embattled defenders of the broken down mission church. The Mexican General, Santa Ana had demanded their surrender, but the occupants of the Alamo knew that the fort was essential to the defense of Texas. Colonel Travis reminded the men, "My orders are to hold this fort. There is no help coming. The Mexicans are 5000 strong." Then Colonel Travis drew a line in the dust with his sword. He said, "Any man who wants to escape is free to go now. Any who are determined to stay and die in defense of the Alamo cross this line." Davy Crockett boldly stepped across the line, the others followed. A few days later, the 232 defenders of the Alamo died in defense of a broken down old mission church. Soon the war cry among Americans was heard, "Remember the Alamo!" That motto fired the Americans on to the final victory over the Mexican forces.

We do not remember the Alamo, but we do remember something far more powerful and sacred: The Last Supper of Jesus Christ. The men of the Alamo were faced with a decision: Would they stand and defend the Alamo? The line was drawn; they crossed that line. We are faced with a decision every day - Will I stand and live my faith? The line is drawn, will I stand and be counted for Christ?

For most of us, Christianity was handed to us when, as babies, we were baptized. But that baptismal commitment must be renewed every day. For us the line is drawn - Will I cross it and live my faith? Or will I escape and live as a practical atheist.

Many who carry the title Christian are practical atheists. Christianity is little more then a title. With their mouth, they do not deny the existence of God, but their lives do. God might as well not exist for them because God does not mean that much to them. How much does God mean to you?

On the First Holy Thursday night, Jesus Christ, God made man, did three things: He washed the feet of the apostles. He gave us His Body and Blood under the appearances of Bread and Wine and instituted the Sacrament of Holy Orders. How important is that to you?

After He washed the disciples' feet Jesus said, "If I washed your feet - I who am Teacher and Lord, then you must wash each other's feet. What I just did was to give you an example. As I have done, so you must do." Jesus doesn't want us to wash one another's feet. What He wants is for us to care about one another, to care about one another so much that if one of us suffers, all of us suffer. If one of us is in need, all of us need to help. If one of us is fortunate, all of us rejoice. The practical atheist cares only about him or herself.

Why does God's command to care for and about one another fall on deaf ears? It falls on deaf ears because God does not exist for the practical atheist. An isolationism, which keeps people separated from one another is godless, is atheistic. Anything that keeps us from having anything to do with one another is godless. God has given us His word, "What I just did, you must do. Care for and about one another."

At every Mass, we see with the eyes of our bodies, simple bread being broken and common wine being poured out. But Jesus reminds us at every Mass, "See, I have broken my Body for you. See, I have poured out my Blood for you. Do This in Remembrance of Me. Break your bodies and pour out your blood by caring for and about one another."

My brothers and sisters: The only hope for our society, the only hope for civilization is this - to live the Mass--to live the Mass by reaching out to one another--by avoiding the godless temptation of seeing life as a struggle for me to get ahead--for me to do my thing and for me to be happy. To live the Mass, to do what Christ has commanded us to do is to make someone else happy, to do someone else's thing to help someone else get ahead. "Do This in Remembrance of Me." This does not mean only to come to Mass ... it means to live the Mass. Breaking our bodies, pouring out our blood with care and concern for one another. This society, our parish and our families rise or fall depending upon our willingness to work together, to care for one another ... to live the Mass.

When the priest stands over the bread and says, "This is My Body," and over the wine says, "This is My Blood." These words should cut deep into our hearts. The words should echo within us. Those words must be our words. With Christ I give myself to others, in humble service. "This is my body broken for you;" these are our words to each other. "This is my blood poured out for you: these are our words to each other.

A practical atheist is one who denies the existence of God, who lives in such a way that it is obvious - God is not important. The manner in which the Christian lives his faith is his commitment to care for and about one another. The only hope for the future of our world, the only hope for the future of a parish, the only hope for the future of your families, our only hope is this: To live our faith, to live the Mass, to care for and about one another - not just in words but in action.

Once again the line is drawn. Are you willing to live your faith? (This is the hour of decision.) Will we live the Mass caring for one another, forgetting ourselves to serve each other? How much does God mean to us really? The line is drawn. Break your bodies, pour out your lives. Let the cry be heard, "Remember Christ. Live the Mass."

A PRIEST'S PRAYER OF THANKSGIVING FOR THE EUCHARIST AND PRIESTHOOD
HOLY THURSDAY -1997

O Jesus, on that First Holy Thursday, gathered in the Upper Room with your disciples, anticipating your death, you left us a memorial, which for all time would put us in conscious contact with you. For every time we gather to celebrate the Eucharist, You are present in our midst, Body, Blood, Soul and Divinity opening the floodgates of Your Heart and flooding us with Your Mercy. We thank you for this great gift, which is the Mass. May we come to appreciate its power and its impact more fully.

We thank you too for the treasure of the priesthood, which you instituted as a special sacrament on the First Holy Thursday. May all priests, who stand at the thousands of altars throughout the world be given a special grace tonight--the grace to be more faithful to you, to be more loving of your church and to be great channels of your mercy to the world. May we all come to dwell more securely and more surely in the folds of your heart - tonight, tomorrow and forever. Amen.

The Eucharist as Communion

CHAPTER 30

I HAVE A DREAM

Martin Luther King gathered with 250,000 before the Lincoln Memorial in Washington, D.C. He deviated from his prepared text and continued, "I have a dream for a country where little white children and little black children can go to the same school. I have a dream today." King's, "I Have A Dream" speech has been one of the most eloquent and one of the most memorable speeches in modern history.

I have a dream. Only human beings can dream, not only in sleeping hours, but also more importantly, during the waking hours. To dream is to set the stage for something better and more beautiful to come. And God has a dream too. From all eternity, God has dreamed of a world kissed with the lips of Divine Love. From the first moments of creation, when humanity was bitten by the snake of rebellion against God, God dreamed of blessing us with serenity and peace. And so His dream became flesh and blood in Jesus, the Christ. Jesus is God's dream come true.

My sisters and brothers, we are in the words of the author Max Lucado one of two things; we are bitten or blessed.

To be bitten means to live in a state or rebellion against God. To live as if God was a nonentity, a nobody. To call our own shots, to think we are our own masters in control of our own destiny and in control of the lives of anybody I can manipulate to do things my way.

To be blessed is to be kissed by the lips of Divine Love. To be blessed is to come to admit that my life has become unmanageable and I need a power greater than myself to help me keep on the straight and narrow--to stay at peace with myself, with God, and with others. That higher power is Jesus--God's dream come true.

We celebrate the Divine Dream in a special way. On Holy Thursday, we are gathered around a banquet table with the Divine Dreamer. Here Jesus reminds us: I have a dream today. I dream of you and I being close friends for life. I dream of your relying on me as your higher power. I can enable you to live with peace within you.

I have a dream! I dream that you will let me guide you, instruct you, heal you, strengthen you, and empower you. I have a dream. I have a dream that you, as my followers, will begin to care for one another to the point of sacrificing your own desires for another's welfare. I dream of you being so filled with my Spirit that you won't ask, "What's in it for me?" before you decide to do something for others, but rather, will spontaneously, give until it hurts. "I have a dream," says the Divine Dreamer.

And on that First Holy Thursday, He showed us what the dream looks like. He bowed low and washed the feet of His followers. Then, He took bread and said, "This is My Body." And He took wine and said, "This is My Blood. Do this in remembrance of me." If you want to follow the dream – do likewise. And, until the end of time, celebrate my dream and yours at future dream feasts, called the Eucharist, the Mass. "Do you understand what I just did for you?" Jesus asked His disciples. "Do you understand the dream?" He asks us. Do you understand? What God wants of us is this, to recognize Him as our personal source.

Dream God's dream; at Mass tell Him, O Jesus, Divine Dreamer, the snake of rebellion has bitten me. Bless me now with the kiss of Divine Love. Help me to dream your dream. You are my higher power and Lord. Thank you for this great gift, the Eucharist. This is your dream fest and I am your special guest. How privileged I am. What a great privilege indeed!

A PRIEST'S HOLY THURSDAY PRAYER

Father, from my mother's womb you have called me by name. And, from all eternity, you have destined me for this service of priesthood. On this day when we commemorate the institution of the sacrament of the Eucharist and the sacrament of priesthood, and are about to celebrate the sacrifice of Your Son in the sacrament of the altar to give you thanks and to ask for continued grace to remain faithful in your service and to be fruitful in your ministry. Fan into flames your spirit-filled gifts and use me for something good, noble and great for you, for your church and for the souls of many. Do not leave me to myself, for without you, all will be brought to destruction. Shepherd my life and make me a shepherd after your own heart. Amen.

The Eucharist as Communion

CHAPTER 31

HOW FIREY IS YOUR FAITH?

Going on pilgrimage to holy places always gives me much to think and pray about. These places, where the Holy is almost touchable, force me to ask myself some important questions.

On my recent pilgrimage, I came to a small country village a few short miles from Medjugorje. Here at the end of World War II when the communists took over Yugoslavia, thirty-five Franciscan Brothers and priests were shot to death. They were given a choice: Life or death. If they wanted to live they had to remove their rosary beads and spit on the crucifix, if they refused, they died. They refused and all were lined up against a stone wall and machine gunned to death. Eyewitness accounts tell how they heard the Franciscans singing while the machine guns rattled around them. The hymn, "Holy God We Praise Thy Name" was heard.

Their bodies were thrown in a fruit cellar and dowsed with kerosene to be burnt, and still the eyewitnesses could hear the faint sound of singing coming from the bullet riddled bodies: "Holy God We Praise Thy Name." The bodies were burnt but the flames of their faith burned brighter than any fire that engulfed their bodies. As I saw the wall and walked through the fruit cellar I asked myself, "how brightly does the fire of my own faith burn?"

The gospel speaks of torches and how important it is to have enough fuel for them. It is a figure of speech. The torch is your faith, the fuel is your love for God. In a time of trial, would you have enough fuel to keep the fire of your faith burning?

While in Rome, at the catacombs, the underground tunnels that provided burial places for the thousands of Christians in the early church, I was forced to face my own weakness. Many early Christians died horrible deaths – decapitation, crucifixion and maybe the most horrible – tied to wooden stakes in the arena of the racetrack, doused with pitch and burned alive to provide lighting for the evening festivities for the emperor and thousands of Romans who came to witness the fun. Those Christians died rather than deny their faith in Christ. If I had lived then, would I have had the courage to die for my faith? I am so weak! Would I choose to die with the faithful or live with the faithless?

A Pope was celebrating Mass in the darkened caverns with a handful of Christians. They knew if they were caught it would mean death, but still they came to worship. The soldiers of the emperor broke in and drug the Pope and his group upstairs and quickly chopped their heads off. The Pope was buried below the very altar he was saying Mass on before he was caught.

Our tour guide at the catacombs was telling us how so many people from former communist countries visit that site where so many faithful Christians are buried. Many of them break down and weep because they understand the risks those Christians took. They understand the price some must pay in order to live their faith. They understand the danger they went through in order to worship their God at Mass.

You and I just can't identify with those who suffer for the faith. We can't fathom how some would take such risks in order to worship. The fact is that we are not challenged to take our faith in Christ as seriously as those who lived in Rome during the persecutions or who have lived or live in communist countries today. We have it so good-we don't know how good we have it.

And yet the eternal choice made by those who were burned in the stadium at Rome or machine gunned by the communists in Medjugorje, is the same choice you and I must make. The choice is made each day, not as dramatically, but the decision is no less momentous, for our eternal salvation or damnation depends on the answer we give to one simple question, "Will I take my faith in Jesus seriously or not?"

One of the most touching moments for me was when we came to a very ancient staircase that led from the underground caverns to the outside. A young man by the name of Tarcisius took that very staircase on the last day of his life. Probably 12 years old, he was given the Blessed Sacrament by the priest, to take to some people in prison; a youngster could have access to the prisoners. But, on his way he encountered a group of pagan boys who noticed Tarcisius was carrying something. They knew it was something Christian and they demanded it. "No!" he said and consumed the Host. He was beaten to death by those boys. He is known as St. Tarcisius, martyr.

Would I have had such a love and devotion for the Blessed Sacrament that I would have died rather than surrender it to the unbelievers? How strongly does the torch of my faith burn?

Those early Christian martyrs would have rather died with the faithful than live with the faithless, so precious was their faith in Jesus. And that faith was not some vague notion, it was a concrete experience they each had of Jesus. Jesus was present to them. They knew Him, they spoke with Him in prayer and because they loved Him so, they would die rather than deny or betray Him...would I?

The pilgrimages challenge me to ask for a greater portion of the fuel of faith to light up my soul. I want what those early martyrs had or what those thirty-five Franciscans had. I want to know, love and believe in Jesus so much that I would rather die then deny Him. If you want this too then join in the hymn that echoes the prayer those thirty-five Franciscans sang as they were machine gunned to death by the communists. A hymn of faith, of love and of hope: Holy God, we praise thy name, Lord of all we bow before Thee. All on earth thy scepter claim, all in heaven above adore Thee. Infinite thy vast domain. Holy, holy, holy is thy reign. Infinite thy vast domain. Holy, holy, holy is thy reign.

The Eucharist as Communion

CHAPTER 32

ONE OF ROME'S GREATEST WONDERS

Most of you have seen pictures of the Coliseum in Rome. Still today one of Rome's greatest wonders, it seated 50,000 spectators. Here the Romans came to see their famous games; lions would entertain the crowds and sometimes water sports were played in the arena. But the main attraction was the shedding of blood--wild beasts tearing each other to pieces and gladiators battling to the death.

The year was 404, the gladiators had entered the arena to the thrill of the crowd; they were ready to fight to the death. Blood would flow like water. Suddenly there was an interruption. A roughly robed man, bareheaded and barefooted springs into the arena waving back at the gladiators. He begins to call aloud upon the people, "Cease the bloodshed...innocent blood must not be shed here." Shouts, cries, boo's and hisses broke in upon his words. "This is no place for preaching. The old customs must be preserved. Back old man...on gladiators!!!" The gladiators threw aside the meddler and rushed for the attack. He still stood between, holding them apart. "Stop," he cried, "No more bloodshed." The mob cried, "Down with him, cut him down." And the gladiators, enraged at the interference, thrust their spears into his heart and stones rained upon him from the crowds above. Then the arena fell silent, the intruder lay dead in the sand. The people came face to face with their own viciousness.

His dress showed that he was a monk who had vowed himself to a life of prayer and self denial. His spirit had been stirred by the sight of thousands flocking to see men slaughter one another and in his simple hearted zeal, he resolved to stop the cruelty or die. He had died, but not in vain. His work was done. The shock of such a death before their eyes turned the hearts of the people. They saw their wickedness and cruelty to which they had blindly surrendered themselves. And since that day when the monk died in the coliseum, there has never been another fight of gladiators. The custom was utterly abolished and one hateful crime at least was wiped from the earth by the self devotion of one humble, obscure and nameless man. This humble, nameless man has courage, something we can all use more of.

Courage comes from two Latin words: cor and agree, heart to do. We need the heart to do what God is asking us to do. To stand up and stand out if need be, for the cause of Christ--to stand up and stand out for the cause of good--to stand up and stand out for faith in a faithless age. Someone once said, "Those who don't stand for something will fall for anything." Too many young people are falling for anything dished out by the media and by a godless education system. Will you be different? Dare to be different!

Whenever you want to understand the spirit of the nameless monk who changed the world think of this fable. Once five fingers stood side by side on a hand, they were all friends. Where one went the others went. They worked together, they played together, they ate and washed, wrote and did their chores together. One day the five fingers were resting on a table together when they spied a gold ring lying nearby. "What a shiny ring." exclaimed the first finger. "It would look good on me," declared the second finger. "Let's take it!" suggested the third finger. "Quick, while nobody's looking," whispered the fourth finger. They started to reach for the ring when the fifth finger, the one named thumb, spoke up, "wait, we shouldn't do that!" it cried. "Why not?" demanded the other four fingers. "Because that ring doesn't belong to us," said the thumb. "It's wrong to take something that doesn't belong to you." "But whose going to know?" asked the other fingers. "No one will see us. Come on, you afraid? What a goody, goody. You're just mad because the ring won't fit you! We thought you were more fun than that!" cried the four fingers. But the thumb shook its head. "I don't care what you say," it answered, "I won't steal!" "Then you can't hang around with us. You can't be our friend," shouted the others. So they went off in a group by themselves and left the thumb alone. At first they thought the thumb would follow them and beg them to take it back, but thumb knew they were wrong and stood fast.

That is why today the thumb stands apart from the other four fingers. Look at your hand. Notice the thumb and ask yourself, "am I willing to stand alone, to stand up, to stand out as a follower of Jesus Christ or not?"

Spend quality time with the best friend you can ever have, Jesus Christ in the Blessed Sacrament. The one who is calling each of you by name is saying, "Come follow Me, come, be my disciple, come-have courage." Who knows, one of you may be like that obscure, nameless man who stood squarely against the power of evil in the coliseum that day so long ago and changed the face of the world. Ask the Lord this weekend, "Could that be me?"

The Eucharist as Communion

CHAPTER 33

TURN DEFEAT INTO VICTORY

An artist decided to paint a man playing chess with the devil. The painting shows the finished game. The devil has won. There are no moves left. The man is depicted staring at the game with terror and horror on his face. That painting hung in a gallery in Europe and many came to see it. All those who understood chess agreed the game was over, the man had no moves left; the devil had checkmated him. Then one day a great master of the game came to see the painting. He ignored all the other pictures in the gallery and studied the chess picture with intense interest. Three, four, five hours passed, and then suddenly he cried out, "It's a lie! The game is not over! The king has another move." The great chess master had seen what no one else had seen. The king had one move left that could change defeat into victory.

Yes, the king always has one move left that can change defeat into victory. The king's name is Jesus, king of kings, lord of lords, and savior of the world. In this time of great national crisis, we need to be reminded of Truth. It is true now, as it always has been, and will be forever: CHRIST CAN CHANGE ANY DEFEAT INTO VICTORY... Romans 8:28. History has ample illustrations of this truth. He writes straight on crooked lines.

The day is October 7th, the year is 1571. Christian Europe has been in a fight for its life with the Islamic invaders for some 700 years. The Christians are preparing for a great naval confrontation with the Turks near a harbor called Lepanto. The prospects of their victory are grim. At the very hour of battle, when the great

Christian fleet was meeting the massive armada of the Turks, the pope, Pope Pius V, far away in a church of Minerva, was leading a procession and praying the rosary. The pope walked to a window, threw open its shutters and stood in a trancelike state for some time. When he returned to his cardinals, he said, "It is now time to give thanks for the great victory which has been granted us. Later it was discovered that the pope's words of victory exactly corresponded to the time when the naval battle was won by the Christians over the Moslem invaders. The pope proclaimed that day, October 7th, from that day forward to be a feast in honor of Mary of the Holy Rosary in gratitude for the victory of that day.

And Jesus says to the apostles in Luke 17, "If you had faith the size of a mustard seed, you could say to this sycamore, be uprooted and transplanted into the sea, and it would obey you."

October 7, 1571 reminds us of the power behind that statement – God can change any defeat into victory. The power is the power of God and the way to tap that power is through prayer. There is something happening in this country and what is happening bodes well in a recent Gallup poll: 64 percent say religion is very important--the highest percentage since 1965. People are beginning to recognize the power of faith and prayer.

For years we have been praying for the change of hearts with regard to abortion, and hearts are being changed. The news reports that the very woman whose abortion rights were legalized in Roe vs. Wade recently was baptized and converted to Christ and the Catholic Church. There is power is prayer, prayer packs a powerful punch. Sometimes a knockout punch.

Let us go back in history again to the battle of Lepanto. After that battle, the Islamic prisoners taken in the battle attested with unmistakable conviction that they had seen Jesus Christ and a multitude of angels in hand fighting against them, blinding them with smoke. The weapon used to win the battle was the rosary. We are <u>not</u> waging war on all the Muslims or the Arabs, no, no, no. What we are waging is a war against the powers of evil wherever they are found. Terrorism is one looming evil, evil bigger than that, but the stench of Satan fills the world in places far and near.

And Christ is calling us to, in the words of St. Paul (Timothy 1), Stir into flame the gift of God, guard the rich deposits of faith with the help of the Holy Spirit who dwells within us. Stir up your faith; pack a powerful punch against evil. Any defeat can become a victory: abortion, stem cell research, cloning, family collapse, violence in schools, abuse, pornography, unbridled pleasure seeking. I invite you to pray, specifically the rosary and when possible to attend daily mass and/or Eucharist adoration at least once a week. Sometimes it seems God is deaf to our pleas. We need a renewed confidence, born of faith: Romans 8:28... Any defeat can be turned into victory through prayer.

A journalist assigned to the Jerusalem bureau takes an apartment overlooking the Wailing Wall. Every day when she looks out, she sees an old Jewish man praying vigorously. So the journalist goes down and introduces herself to the old man. She asks, "You come everyday to the wall. How long have you done that and what are you praying for?" The old man replies, "I have come here to pray everyday for 25 years. In the morning I pray for world peace and then for the brotherhood of man. I go home have a glass of tea, and I come back and pray for the eradication of illness and disease from the earth." The journalist is amazed. "How does it make you feel to come here everyday for 25 years and pray for these things?" she asks. The old man looks at her sadly. "I feel like I'm talking to a wall, but I know God is listening." Sometimes we feel we are just talking to a wall- -our prayers going unheard. But, in faith we know God always hears the prayers of a sincere heart. Our faith can change defeat into victory.

When we come to the celebration of the Mass, we are participating in the great victory of Christ. Through His Passion, death and resurrection, Christ has given us all a share in this victory of life over death. When you encounter the Crucified and Risen Savior in Holy Eucharist, or when you spend time before the Blessed Sacrament, take time to review your life. In this most intimate communion with the Savior, let Him remind you that any defeat, no matter how devastating, can become a victory. History proves it, our faith proclaims it, and prayers produce it.

The Eucharist as Communion

CHAPTER 34

KING OF HEARTS

In the Holy Land, along the Via Dolorosa, the cobblestone walkway which leads from Pilate's Palace to the mount called Calvary, there is a small church. It marks the spot where Christ was scourged at the pillar. On the tabernacle of this small chapel, on the door of it, there are the words KING OF HEARTS printed. King of Hearts, now that is what the Mass is all about. The Eucharist is the event of the tender meeting of the heart of man with the King of Hearts.

The solemnity of Corpus Christi is the feastday honoring the body of Christ in the Holy Eucharist. It is the King of Heart's feastday. Since Christ is the King of hearts and the Eucharist, the Mass is the tender meeting of our hearts with His. What is it that this meeting does for us and to us? To celebrate the Mass as it should be requires something of us. It requires that we come into God's presence with open hands and open hearts.

There are many things in our lives to which we cling with a clenched fist: our possessions for sure, our work, our careers, the friends we have and our self-image. We cling also to our memories, sometimes involving our resentments, our unforgiven mistakes, our hurts and our guilt.

When we open our hand before God, we become vulnerable. That's what the Mass is: becoming vulnerable before God. When we open our hands with all that we have and are resting there, the Lord will come and look and roam through our hands to see what we have there. Then a tender meeting of hearts occurs.

Then Christ looks at me and asks, "Would you mind if I take out this little bit?" What would you answer? And perhaps the Lord will look another time at me and ask: "Would you mind if I put something else in your hands?" Now what's your answer? This is the heart of the Mass. The King of hearts meets me and in this meeting of hearts, God may take something and He may put something in. It's my choice!

I remember a youngster who used to love to hold on to his little coins, tightly rapping those few coins in his clenched fist. When you tried to coax him to open his hand to show you his treasure, he would hold up his fist and cry out, "Mine." One day he was exceedingly tight fisted with his possessions, until a five dollar bill was flashed before his greedy little face. Boy did that hand fly open, like an electric door. It's the same with us.

We hold on tight to the things we possess until we come to a realization that something far greater and far more valuable is being flashed before our faces. That's what the Mass is.

We come tight fisted holding on to our material possessions, our relationships, our health, our hopes, our dreams, and the Lord invites us to open up. And in order to coax us a little, He shows us His heart. That bleeding gaping wound in the side of Christ's chest reveals His heart, open and inviting. O my Jesus, you have not refused to give me your blood and your life. How then can I refuse to give you my miserable heart?

In the gospel story, the disciples gave Jesus the little they had: five loaves and two fishes, and the crowd was fed to the point that twelve baskets were left over. That event was an image of what happens at Mass.

We come with the little we have: our needs, our hopes, our mistakes, our sorrows, our questions, our frustrations, and our hurts. We come with our possessions, our relationships, our past, with its sins and then we open our hands to give Him what we have and what we are, just like the disciples gave Jesus all that they had. Then at the Mass the Lord gives us 100 fold back, but what often happens is we come tight fisted revealing to the Lord the little we want to show Him. We hold back from Him some possession that we do not want Him to have. We keep tightly clenched in our fists perhaps a relationship we wish not to change or give up. We hold on tight to some habit, some attitude, and some way of acting we wish not to give up. And so we leave as miserly and closed, untouched and unmoved, as we came. Do you live six days a week as if Sunday and God never existed? Some do--because they're too clenched fisted with God.

Imagine placing all that you possess, all your personal property, in your hand. Now add all your ways of thinking and acting, all your relationships, all that you have been and are, right there in the palm of your hand. Would you open it up and offer it to God seeing that He could remove whatever He chose and replace whatever He wanted? Hard to do? But that is what this Mass is all about. O loving heart of Jesus, it is now up to you to make wholly yours this poor heart which in the past has been so ungrateful. Inflame this heart with your love, as your heart burns with love for me. The Lord will always replace more than He takes. He is generous and compassionate and cannot be outdone in his generosity. Once we open up our lives to Him, we begin to love with a new love.

During the early part of World War II, the North Atlantic battle zone became knows as torpedo junction. German submarines preyed relentlessly on American ships, sending men and material to an icy grave. For awhile these U-Boats, operating in wolf packs, sank an average of 100 ships per month. In January 1943, an old ship known as the Dorchester slipped her New England moorings and heaved for Europe. On board were four chaplains, one Catholic, two Protestants and one Jewish. They had their work cut our for them. When February 2nd rolled around, a Coast Guard cutter blinked a signal that the convoy was being followed by an enemy sub. Nothing could be done, except hope and pray. Suddenly at 1:00 a.m., a torpedo ripped into the side of the Dorchester and exploded with terrific force. Steam lines broke and men were scalded before they could abandon ship. In the darkness and confusion, a soldier cried out, "I've lost my life jacket." No one knows who was first, but one of the chaplains gave his life jacket away. As the Dorchester listed heavily in her final moments, the four chaplains found each other. Each had given his life jacket to one of the men. They stood on the slanted deck, with arms around each other, praying just before their own death.

Now that is real caring, that's loving that can come only from the bleeding heart of Jesus. That's the kind of loving God wants from us, but that can only happen if we understand the Mass. What is the Mass? Look at the cross, the open side, open heart – a meeting of hearts. The mass is a tender meeting of our heart with Christ's, the King of hearts. When we go to communion, imagine all you have and are, being held up before God, open that hand to Christ, mystically, truly present under appearance of bread and wine. He'll give more than He'll ever take. At the conclusion of Mass, a simple procession with the Blessed Sacrament through Church. Remember Christ, King of Hearts, comes to us as simple bread – meets us in the Mass. Will we open up our hands and hearts to Him?

The Eucharist as Communion

CHAPTER 35

WHAT IS THE MASS?

What is the Mass? If someone approached you with that question, what would you say? In the tradition of the Church, we describe the Mass as sacrifice and sacrament. What does that mean?

Allow me to use an illustration – During the Vietnam War several mortar rounds landed in a small village, some hitting an orphanage. Several missionaries and some of the children were killed outright and many others wounded, including one young girl, about eight years old, who had suffered wounds to her legs. In a nearby hospital the little girl was being treated. A blood transfusion was imperative, but supplies of plasma were limited and a matching blood type was required. The doctor explained to the frightened children survivors that unless they could replace some of their friend's lost blood, she would certainly die. Then the doctor asked if anyone would be willing to give some of their blood to help. The request was met with wide-eyed silence. The little child's life was in the balance. Only if one of these frightened children volunteered could she live. After several long moments, a little hand slowly and waveringly went up, dropped back down, and after a moment went up again. A little child came forward. He was quickly laid on a pallet and the needle inserted in his vein. Through the ordeal, the child lay still, silent and wide-eyed. After a moment, he let out a shuddering sob, quickly covering his face with his free hand. "Is it hurting?" "No," whimpered the child. After a few more moments, another sob escaped and again he covered up his face crying. "Does it hurt?" "No."

Again the same thing happened, a whimper, a sob and a cry. The doctor became concerned and so he called for an interpreter. The nurse spoke to the child stroking his forehead. Then the nurse said quietly to the American doctor: "This child thought he was dying. He misunderstood you. He thought you had asked him to give all his blood so the little girl could live." "But why would he be willing to do that?" asked the doctor. The Vietnamese nurse repeated the question to the little boy, who answered simply, "She's my friend."

A little Vietnamese orphan, a tragic mortar attack, and an unselfish act of love and bravery stir our hearts and challenge our minds to a deeper understanding of the Mass. The mass is a sacrifice. As the little orphan unselfishly laid his life on the line for another, so Christ laid His life on the cross for us so that by His blood our sins might be washed away. He died so we might live eternally. The mass is a representation of this sacrifice of the cross. It is as if the cross of Calvary is uprooted and planted squarely in our midst so that we may draw nigh unto it allowing that trickling of Christ's life-giving Blood to wash us clean to give us new life. Though your sins are as scarlet, they shall be white as snow. Though they be red as crimson, they shall be white as wool. This is the Mass, an eternal sacrifice. Though offered once on Calvary, its effects endure throughout time and are made present at the Mass.

On the hillside on the shore of Tiberius, Jesus fed the five thousand. Jesus took five barley loaves of bread and a couple of dried fish and fed the multitudes. At every Mass, the Lord feeds us with His own Body and Blood so that our hunger for healing, our need for freedom from sin may be satisfied. The Mass is a sacrifice because it represents the saving act of Calvary. It is a sacrament because at it we eat the very Body and Blood of Christ.

If we look briefly at the structure of the Mass, we see how the twofold nature of the Mass, sacrifice and sacrament, stand out in bold relief. In the first half of the Mass, the liturgy of the Word, we hear the Lord address us directly. Through the Bible readings, the Lord calls us to conversion, to repentance, to turn our back on sin and turn toward Him and His mercy. And then in the second part of the Mass, the liturgy of the Eucharist, we join our hearts and minds in a great prayer of thanksgiving to God for saving us in Christ. This prayer invites us to place ourselves on the altar and then with Jesus to offer ourselves to our Heavenly Father and through our union with Jesus on the altar we are lifted up as Jesus was lifted up on the cross. We are set free to live a more God-centered life. Then in Holy Communion we are joined most intimately with the Savior and empowered by Him to live a changed existence.

The Mass is sacrifice and sacrament because of what Christ has done for us and continues to do for us, even to this day. The Mass is sacrifice and sacrament because Christ wants us to sacrifice ourselves with Him on the altar.

Notice in the gospel the lad who sent only a few loaves and fishes to Christ, but it was plenty because it was presented to Jesus. Jesus needs us to bring Him all that we have and are too. The fact of faith is that Jesus needs what we can bring Him at Mass. We may not have much to bring, but He needs what we have. Little is always much in the hand of Christ.

The problem often is cited that people don't go to Mass because they don't get anything from it. The problem is not with the Mass. The problem is with that person because we get from the Mass only in proportion to what we bring to it. If we bring our struggles against sin and place them on the altar, we will leave conquerors. If we bring our loneliness and present it to Christ on the altar, we leave filled with His presence. If we give up our addictions and present at the altar giving Christ our unsavory inordinate passion for booze, drugs, sex, money, clothing or food, we will leave empowered to cope in constructive, not destructive, ways. If we bring our joys and sorrow, our hopes and fears and consciously present them to Christ on this altar, then we will find our hopes renewed, our fears allayed, our sorrows ceasing and our dreams becoming reality.

What is the Mass? It is a sacrifice, Christ's and ours. It is a sacrament. It holds out to us the hope of a changed, a healed, a transformed and a renewed life. But we receive only in proportion to what we bring to the Mass.

Remember the story of the little Vietnamese orphan. It is a story of a tragic mortar attack and an unselfish sacrifice of love and bravery which stirs our hearts and challenges our minds. It is a challenge to understand the Mass. It is a challenge to love the Mass and to live it.

The Eucharist as Communion

CHAPTER 36

HUNGER PAINS

Someone once described a priest as one beggar showing other beggars where to find bread. Good description. Our world is having great hunger pains and for many, the hunger pains have persisted for so long that they are numbed by the pain and they no longer realize how desperate their condition is. People are hungry for God and many don't even realize it. In the words of St. Augustine, our hearts are restless and they shall not rest until they rest in God. Our souls are hungry and they shall not be satisfied until they are filled with God. What do these hunger pains feel like? Our hunger for God reveals itself in that deep gnawing need for companionship. We have all been made for God and within us is an empty space only God can fill. That empty space is a cry for companionship, divine friendship, and intimacy with God.

I heard this saying, "Show me your friends and I will show you your future." If you want to know what your future will look like, search that space deep within your soul where only God can dwell. Do you have a companion in your God? Do you meet with Jesus to discuss your life's issues, your joys and sorrows, hopes and fears? If you do, your future has hope.

The feast of Corpus Christi reminds us to look at our companionship with Christ. Have I let Jesus occupy that special place in my soul? I think the reason the Lord chose bread and wine as the sacramental way He could share Himself with us was in order to point to the fact that He wants to enter into our souls, deep within. But the Eucharist is stripped of much of its meaning if we don't realize what we are doing when we receive Communion. We are opening our hearts to God in order for Him to take up residence there. This is no mere symbol you are receiving here. This is no mere reminder of a supper held so long ago by Jesus and the twelve. The bread and wine you receive are not mere tokens of God's love. They are His love. They are Jesus Himself, communicating Himself as food for our souls.

A recent survey tells a terrible tale of failing faith for many Catholics today. Survey results: only one-third believe in the Orthodox Catholic teaching on the Eucharist. So many fail to fathom the meaning of what they do here at every Mass. Not so throughout the whole world. There is a group that has no misgivings about the meaning of what appears to be a simple wafer of bread and a sip of wine. This group knows of the power of the Eucharist. This group stands in awe of it so much so that it does everything it can to undermine the Mass and its sacredness. Who is this group? It is the devil worshippers, Satanists. They go to great lengths in their black masses, to desecrate the Mass. It knows of the power of the Sacred Host. These Satanists sometimes try to steal the Blessed Sacrament. Why? Because they have no doubts, these devil worshippers, that this is the true Body, Blood, Soul and Divinity of Jesus Christ, Son of God and Savior of the world. They have turned their backs on God and there is no room for Him in their soul, only darkness and despair and deviousness.

This world hungers for peace, serenity and love, but it refuses to accept the food that God has given us to feed our starving spirits. It refuses to accept the Bread of Life in the Eucharist, even some Catholics have fallen for the lie that love and serenity can be found without God.

In Betania, Venezuela a Eucharistic miracle occurred a few years ago. A priest celebrated Mass at Betania Shrine and the Host began to bleed. The Bishop investigated the case and found it to be true human blood. It is a reminder to a faithless age, this is no mere bread. It is really Jesus.

Why have outdoor Eucharistic processions? An outdoor procession is a simple gesture reminding the world, all who care to look, that Jesus is the only answer to the hungering soul. He is the Divine companion for our walk through life. He alone has the key to serenity and peace for your heart. I am one beggar showing other beggars where to find bread, the Bread of Eternal Life. Receive Him in the Eucharist and tell Him, "You, O Jesus, are my Savior and Lord. Feed my soul with your love and let nothing take your place in my heart"

A DEDICATION OF FAITH IN THE REAL PRESENCE: Soul of Christ sanctify me; Body of Christ save me; Blood of Christ inebriate me; Water from the side of Christ, wash me; O passion of Christ strengthen me; O good Jesus hear me; Within thy wounds hide me; From the wicked enemy defend me; And at the hour of my death call me; And bid me come to Thee, that with thy saints I may praise you forever. Amen."

The Eucharist as Communion

CHAPTER 37

WHO ARE YOU?

The actor known as Mr. T. was reflecting about his mother and who she was to him. He said he wanted to recognize her hands, her feet, and her knees. He wanted to recognize her feet because they had taken her across town to do domestic work--her hands and knees scrubbing floors and toilets. "It was my mother," he said, "who walked the floor with me on her feet all night long, talking to God. Then she would get down on her knees to pray some more, still holding me in her hands. My mother was God sent." Mr. T's mother knew who God created her to be.

In the gospel, John the Baptizer realized who he was too. A voice crying in the wilderness, "Make straight the way of the Lord." Do you know who you are? Some of the saddest people in the world are those who hate who they are. Looking constantly to be like someone else. Listen! We need to remember that God doesn't make mistakes. When He created you, He knew what He was doing. The problem is not with God, it's with us. When we feel insecure, unsure of ourselves, walking in a fog of uncertainty, we need to look at Christ and remind ourselves, God doesn't make junk, and He knew what He was doing when I was made. Not just a social security number, a consumer, a customer, a voter or a worker, but a precious creation in God's spirit.

The Mass itself is a reminder to us of who we are. Let's look at it for a moment. We begin every Mass with a procession of the priest and servers to the altar. We are in procession, moving towards heaven. That's what we are from cradle to grave, either heaven or hell. We continue the Mass with a sign of the cross and the Lord have mercy. We are marked men and marked women. Christ has signed us with His cross at baptism. Who are we? We are His very own and yet we are sinners. Lord, have mercy, forgive us. Let us pray, the priest announces. As created people, God wants us to talk to Him. We are prayerful people. We listen then to the words of the Bible. We have much to learn from God. We are listeners, hearers of the Word of God. That word must touch our minds, our mouths and our hearts. We profess our faith in the creed. We must be people of faith. This ends the first part of the Mass. We have been reminded of who God created us to be: pilgrims; His people; marked men; in need of mercy; listeners; people of faith.

The first part of the Mass is called the Liturgy of the word. The second is called the Liturgy of the Eucharist, which included the great prayer of thanksgiving. We begin here with the presentation of the gifts, the bread and wine, the offering of money. God has made us for Himself. By presenting our gifts, we present ourselves. We are God's people; all that we have is His. "Let us give thanks to the Lord our God," the priest intones. We are created to be thankful people. In the great prayer which follows, we praise God for all His gifts, especially the gift of Jesus and the fact that He died on the cross for us and has sent His spirit among us. During the solemn proclamation of the Eucharistic Prayer by the priest, the bread and wine are changed into the Body and Blood of Christ. Christ's presence in history is acknowledged with gratitude, and His presence under the signs of Bread and Wine is proclaimed in a solemn prayer of praise. And so, we are people of thanks, through Christ, with Christ, in Christ. Through the words of this prayer of praise, we unite ourselves to Christ's sacrifice—extended through time and made mystically present on the altar. We pray the primordial Christian prayer together, "Our Father." God is our father; we are his sons and daughters. When we receive communion the priest pronounces these words: "The Body of Christ, Amen. The Blood of Christ, Amen." With these words we receive Communion. Here God teaches us in a most personal way who we are. We are part of His Body, His Church. Saint Augustine reminds us: "Become what you receive." We must more perfectly become united to Christ, the Head of the Body, so that we can more lovingly embrace the Body of Christ, which is His Church. We are together called to be the holy people He created us to be. "The Mass is ended, Go in Peace," the deacon chants. These words can well be called, "the great sending," for we are now sent forth, to proclaim our identity as members of Christ's Body, the Church. We are filled again with the divine presence of God. People of Christ's peace, thankful disciples of the Lord—we are creatures of God called to holiness, this is what the second part of the Mass tells us about who we are. We have no need to want to be anyone else because God has made each of us unique, special, worthy of His love—but all sharing a common destiny in Christ—eternal life. "Ite Missa est," Go, you are sent forth. Proclaim the Good News!!!

During the Vietnam War a young husband had to leave his bride one week after their wedding day. Although they were half a world apart, she in Iowa, he in Vietnam, letters flew frequently across the sea. Now and then a gift told of their devotion. Eagerly they waited for these messages and gifts. Fondly they read and reread them. Then suddenly, late one night, the young wife heard a loud knock at the door. Cautiously, she opened to see her soldier husband standing there with a grin that reached from ear to ear. As they embraced, they laughed and cried with joy. Do you think that young wife spent any time that evening reading the messages or looking over the gifts he had sent her? No, she looked at him. She talked to him. She threw her arms about him again and again. He was home. He was really here. And God is really here at this Mass. We not only remember His coming two thousand years ago, we relive it because Christ is really here to tell us again, I love you, you are mine.

The Eucharist as Communion

CHAPTER 38

WORRY

Some of us are champion worriers. There once was an elderly shopkeeper who was on his deathbed surrounded by his family. He feebly asked, "Is Sara here?" "Yes, I'm here," said his wife. "Is Ruth here?" he asked. "Yes, daddy." "And, Bill?" "Yes, father." Then the old man sat up with terror in his eyes and yelled, "Then who's mending the store?"

No matter how good things seem to be, we'll find something to worry about. Sometimes we think we have to worry in order to get things done. Worry for many is a tool to control and manage our lives. Worry can become a habit, but habits can be broken. The worry trap can hold us in bondage for a lifetime, keeping us imprisoned in a jail of our own making.

At the heart of this addiction to worry is a lack of faith because when we think we have to worry in order to live, we are forgetting who is really in charge of this universe, and it isn't you or I. What the worrier needs is less self-control and more God control. The gospel speaks to us of the one valuable pearl which a man found in field. It was so valuable that he sold everything in order to purchase that field. For many of us, there is a treasure buried in our lives which we need to rediscover. It is this: faith letting God mind the store and letting Him do the worrying. That's not easy for us habitual addicted worriers, but if we are to understand the peace that Jesus wishes us to have, we have to surrender our old ways of coping, namely giving over to God control of our lives. Someone once put it this way, life is like a trip in an automobile. We are so used to doing all the driving; it seems crazy to turn loose the steering wheel. But God is a good driver. He'll steer us along the right road.

The English word worry is derived from an Anglo-Saxon word, *woriern*, that means "to strangle" or "to choke". Worry cuts off the air supply that allows us to accept the gift which is today. People get so busy worrying about yesterday or tomorrow that they miss today. An old woman who had a habit of worrying used to say, "I always feel bad when I feel good because I just know that I'll feel bad after a while."

Worry chokes off the air flow of the Holy Spirit, robbing us of the grace of each day. One of the ways to deal with our worries is the way described in a story about Babe Ruth. Babe had fallen away from his Catholic religion and at one point in his career he took deadly sick. He was worried. This could be the end – career, life, all. Lying in a New York hospital bed, Paul Carey, one of Babe's oldest friends asked, "Babe, they're going to operate in the morning. Don't you think you should see a priest?" Ruth realized that death could strike him out, so he agreed. That night Babe Ruth spends a long time talking to Jesus with the priest's assistance. When he finished, Babe made a full confession. After the priest left, Babe knew he had nothing to worry about. All was in God's hands. Are worries choking off the air flow of the Holy Spirit, robbing you of the peace Jesus won for you on the cross? Do you need to turn over the steering wheel of your life to Christ and make a fresh start of a real life of trusting God? Then, today is the day to do it. This very Mass may be the beginning of a new chapter in your life--a chapter of serenity and peace. But what we must do is really let Christ take over for us. John Paul, the prophet said, "Do not despair. God always wins in the end."

As the soldier left for the war, he told his wife he'd be back soon. He was off to fight in World War II, leaving his family behind. Five years went by. The young mother would show her son a portrait of the soldier and say, "See, that's your daddy. One day he's going to come home." In reality, she really didn't know what to expect. One morning, the boy said, "Mommy, wouldn't it be great if daddy would just step out of the picture frame?"

In a sense, that's what God did two thousand years ago. As part of his eternal plan, He stepped out of heaven and became man so you and I could look at Jesus and say, "That's what God looks like." And that's what happens at Mass. You look at the cross and you see His love and mercy, but the Mass is more than just gazing at an inanimate image of an impotent God. The Mass is God's stepping out of the lifeless image of the crucifixion and becoming real and touchable here and now, so that at the Mass, we can really turn over to Him the steering wheel of our lives and trust Him to steer us along the highways and by-ways of life. Let worry be a thing of the past.

As an old hymn puts it: "What a friend we have in Jesus. All my sins and grieves to bear. What a privilege to carry everything to God in prayer. O what peace we often forfeit. O what needless pain we bear. All because we do not carry everything to God in prayer. Have we trials and temptations? Is there trouble anywhere? We should never be discouraged. Take it to the Lord in prayer. Can we find a friend so faithful, who will all our sorrows, share? Jesus knows our every weakness. Take it to the Lord in prayer."

Conclusion

LITURGY OF THE WORD, LITURGY OF THE EUCHARIST

One day a young student approached the great philosopher Socrates with this complaint, "Teacher, you are always saying the same thing. Socrates replied, "If I am asked what is 2 x 2, am I not to say the same thing?" Truth is eternal, unchanging. The truths of the Catholic faith are old, as old as Christianity, but there are new listeners who need these truths and there are also old listeners who need to have their memories refreshed. One of these truths is the Mass.

Sometimes when the routine of weekly Mass and the apparent repetitiveness of the ceremony and words get us down, we need to remind ourselves of the timelessness and unchangeableness of the mystery of faith we celebrate at every Mass. The truth of the Mass remains untouched by time. The language, the ceremony may change, but the mystery of it is eternal.

Like the crowds gathered on the grass before Jesus in the gospel, we are invited to listen to Him teaching us about the Bread of Life and to receive this Bread, which is His body with renewed awareness. What I would like to do is to look again at the mystery of the Mass in order to unlock the priceless treasure of unchangeable truth contained in it. The Mass began over 19 centuries ago in an upper room in Jerusalem. There seated with his 12 apostles, Jesus and His followers sang hymns and listened to the scripture. Then Jesus gave thanks to God the Father. Blessed bread and wine, broke the bread and gave to his disciples saying, "Take and eat. Take and drink. This is my Body. This is my Blood." Then they ate and drank. "Do this in memory of me," Jesus said. In that brief outline is found the basic structure of the Mass.

Faithful to Jesus' command, we gather together like the disciples in the upper room. First we hear God's word, liturgy word, and then we partake of the Word of Life, Jesus, by being taken up with Him in an act of praise and thanksgiving to the heavenly Father. This act of praise culminates in our receiving Jesus Himself in communion, liturgy of the Eucharist.

There are two basic parts to the Mass: liturgy of the word and liturgy of the Eucharist. Let's look at the basic structure. We assemble as God's people, singing hymns in praise of Father, Son and Spirit. We then acknowledge our need for God and our unworthiness in the penitential prayers. "I confess" and "Lord have mercy," then the Gloria, a song of praise is sung. Closing the introductory part of the Mass is the opening prayer. It collects our sentiments in an initial approach to God, petitioning Him for a deeper faith. Then the word of God is addressed to us in three Bible readings, homily, creed, and prayer of faithful. The liturgy of the word, first part of Mass, attempts to help us know who Jesus was, why He came to save us, and how we can be united with Him. It also prepares us in faith for Part 2, when Jesus' presence is renewed and He is given to us as food.

After the presentation of gifts by representatives of the congregation, gifts are placed on the altar. This begins the liturgy of the Eucharist. These gifts represent you and the offering of yourselves to God with His Divine Son. Shortly, the priest begins the most solemn prayer of the Eucharist, the great thanksgiving prayer, with lift up your hearts, let us give thanks to the Lord our God. This is a summary of our attitude, with hearts uplifted; we give thanks to God for his gifts of salvation in Christ. Throughout this long Eucharist prayer, note the many times the word "thanks" is used. This prayer, thanks God for His saving love in Christ, the cross and resurrection. Through the Eucharist prayer we ask the Father to send the Holy Spirit into our midst, changing bread and wine into the Body and Blood of Christ, and also to change us into Christ's holy people. At the end of the Eucharist prayer, the priest is seen raising Body and Blood upward; our prayers and praise, ourselves ascend to the Father through Christ, with Christ, and in

Christ, all glory and honor is God the Father's forever. Then we solemnly sing the "Great Amen." We are proclaiming our "Yes, I believe all that has been proclaimed in the Eucharistic Prayer."

After the Our Father, during Lamb of God, the bread of heaven is broken. Mass used to be called the "breaking of the bread." Symbolism here is rich; as Christ was broken on the cross for us, so this bread, His Body, is broken and shared so that we may take part in the saving grace won for us on the cross. As bread is broken, so we must break ourselves in love for others. At Communion, when we say Amen, we are saying yes, Lord, I want to be a part of your Body, the Church. Then there are the Closing prayer and a blessing.

The second part of the Mass reenacts a miracle before which all other are nothing. The saving grace of the cross and resurrection are ours in the gift Christ in Holy Communion.

St. Francis sums up the ineffable mystery and grandeur of the Mass. He speaks to us: "The mystery of the Mass is of tremendous grandeur. May every person stand in awe, may the whole world tremble, may heaven exult when Christ, the Son of the living God is on the altar in the hands of the priest. O admirable grandeur and marvelous goodness. O sublime humility and humble sublimity. The master of the universe, God and Son of God, humbles Himself for our salvation. See the humility of God-- you too must humble yourselves in order to be exalted by Him. Keep nothing for yourselves, nothing of yourselves, give all to God, that you may be able to receive entirely Him who gives Himself to you entirely."

Why is the Mass always the same? If I am asked what 2 x 2 is, am I not always to say the same thing? The truth of the Mass is eternal, unchanging. Can we ask for anything more?

"What the senses fail to fathom, let us grasp through faith's consent!" (St. Thomas Aquinas)